ENDORSEMENTS FOR *THE NINE SPIRITUAL FRONTS*

I have known Danny Thornton as a gifted pastor and evangelist for over thirty years. I have also come to know him as vibrant member of our ministerial network and a dear friend. This book blew me away. Danny has written the finest book on the fruit of the Spirit I have ever encountered. His insights are simultaneously convicting and inspiring. Danny's skillful writing draws the reader through a journey that exposes the heart of a God who calls us to share in his holy nature. I am giving this book to every leader in our Network.

John Carter
Lead Pastor, Abundant Life Christian Center
Director, Abundant Life Ministerial Network

Many Christians want more of God, more of His presence. But some may want to be transformed into His glorious image, and be able to get out of God's way and let Him flow through you. This book gives insights into how God can work and live through you! It is an interesting and fun read. Enjoy this book and enjoy the Lord!

Rev Barbara Marang
Pastor/Missionary to Honduras

I have had the privilege of watching Danny Thornton grow from a new-born Christian into a very successful Pastor, and through his ministry many lives have been changed. God provided these Nine Spiritual Fronts to keep us balanced, successful and spiritually healthy. This book will open your understanding so you can utilize them all. You'll be blessed by this book—Danny not only wrote it but lives it as well.

James Roger Farley
Founding Pastor, Family Worship Center, Clay NY

I am excited about this book and the effect it will have on believers and on churches. It comes at a time when people need clear and direct instruction concerning the Holy Spirit and His purposes in a person's life. Danny has not just taught these principles but lived them. I highly recommend this book to you and know that you will be inspired and enriched by it.

Andy Elmes
Senior Pastor, Family Church, Portsmouth, UK

The Nine Spiritual Fronts is certainly one of the clearest and most useful resources we have ever seen! This book is literally 'dripping' with years of ministry experience and godly wisdom. Each chapter is like opening a beautiful 'gift of enrichment', a treasure trove of usable truths. Thank you, Danny, for your gift of 'revelation information' that is sure to bless many richly. It will be a lasting resource and 'go-to' text for years to come. Blessings in Jesus!

Dr. Len and Cathy Mink
evangelists, singers and TV presenters

I am so pleased for Danny to see his dream of writing a book come to pass, it's been a long time coming. Yet this book only scratches the surface of the depth and richness of the wisdom that God has cultivated in Danny's heart, so I know this won't be the only book he writes. I've known Danny for many years, and his heart is only to grow and empower people to be who God made them to be. He believes in people, he releases them, he keeps them grounded and focused. This book has been a joy to read.

Matt Lockwood
Worship Pastor, Family Church, Portsmouth, UK

THE

9

SPIRITUAL FRONTS

THE

9

SPIRITUAL FRONTS

Living an empowered life through the Fruit of the Spirit

Danny Thornton

This edition published in 2018 by Great Big Life Publishing
Empower Centre, 83-87 Kingston Road, Portsmouth, PO2 7DX, UK.

British Library Cataloguing in Publication Data. A catalogue record for this book is available from the British Library.

Cover concept: Zefanya Nadia Putri
Photo by Alessio Soggetti on Unsplash.com
ISBN-13: 978-0-9957925-8-6
ISBN-10:
eBook ISBN: 978-0-9957925-9-3

CONTENTS

DEDICATION

I WANT to sincerely thank my lovely bride, Jean Marie, for being an incredible and faithful wife and friend, going on for fifty years. Shout outs also go out to my loving daughters, Shannon and Danielle, and two great son-in-laws (sons-in-grace!), Dan and Tim, and not forgetting the best grandchildren a Papa could ever ask for: Arianna, Kaylah, Moriah, Daniel, Caleb and Ava.

Thanks for loving me—it is my heart-felt prayer that you will pass the baton of Christian legacy onto your loved ones.

Finally, I give thanks to God and the Lord Jesus Christ.

FOREWORD

I AM very excited about this fantastic book by my friend Danny Thornton. He has been a dear friend of mine and my family's for many years now, and from that long-term relationship I can tell you that in this book are distilled the wisdom, thoughts and revelations of a man who has walked faithfully and served God passionately for many years. Through good and tough seasons I have seen Danny continually and relentlessly pursue God and His ways. He is a very humble man, not scared of change or to reinvent things when needed. He consistently demonstrates wisdom and faithfulness in his relationships and ministry to all people, regardless of whether they be close friends or strangers.

This book comes at a time when people need clear and direct instruction concerning the Holy Spirit and His purposes in a person's life. Danny digs deep into very simple yet profound truths concerning the ministry of the Spirit, giving great revelation concerning the nine spiritual fruit that are listed in Galatians. To describe them as nine spiritual 'fronts' is genius because it is so true – these nine areas are where we experience the greatest warfare, because they are also the means through which we can experience God's great kingdom manifesting and establishing itself upon the earth. If the enemy can cause these areas – these nine avenues through which the character of God can be witnessed to His creation – to be hindered, confused, misguided, misunderstood, or even broken, then this world will continue along the path of destruction and darkness that it has been set upon, without knowing the true nature of God or coming to the understanding of His great salvation. Using many real life examples and testimonies, Danny opens up these nine 'fronts' in such a way that things you thought you knew are suddenly revealed in a new and fresh way. There is a lot of wisdom within this book for the person who seeks it – wisdom that comes from revelation the Lord has given Danny and from things he has learned through faithfully following the Lord over many years.

With opportunities to pause for thought and reflection, and to stop and pray about things you have read, spread throughout the book, Danny has written in a wonderful way that it is very easy to read. Yet I would encourage you to not speed read it but to take time to think and digest the truths captured within.

Danny has not just taught these principles but modeled them for his church and his friends to see. I know that you will be inspired and enriched by it. Well done, Danny, I know that being obedient to God and writing this book was a new challenge for you but you did it, my friend, and you did it so well! It is such a good read, and a very empowering one too. Love you, my friend.

Andy Elmes
Senior Pastor, Family Church, UK

THE FRUIT OF THE SPIRIT

"But the fruit of the Spirit is love, joy, peace, long-suffering, gentleness, goodness, faith, meekness, temperance: against such there is no law."
Galatians 5:22-23

"So, I say, let the Holy Spirit guide your lives. Then you won't be doing what your sinful nature craves."
Galatians 5:16 (NLT)

THE HIGHEST moral code that exhibits godly character and virtue can be found in the Bible, where it lists nine Fruits of the Spirit (Galatians 5:22-

23). Most Bible scholars believe these are the godly characteristics that Jesus exhibited during His time here on earth.

One would think that every believer would have a burning desire to live a life that exemplifies the character of Christ and leaves a healthy, spiritual legacy behind him or her. Unfortunately, that is not always the case for a number of reasons. One of those reasons is that some believers are ignorant regarding how to tap into these powerful virtues on a daily basis. This is where the Holy Spirit, our Helper, comes in.

Without the leading of our Helper, the Holy Spirit, it is impossible to bear fruit. Now if we will allow the Holy Spirit to guide our lives, we won't give in as often to what our sinful nature craves. This is the reason why the Holy Spirit made His home in us at the second birth, our salvation. When we became born-again, the Holy Spirit indwelled within our human spirit and these powerful virtues flooded our spirit with His character.

So, how do we tap into these nine spiritual fruits? John the Baptist gave us a hint about how to do this saying, "He must increase, but I must decrease." (John 3:30) So the formula seems quite simple: It is less of us and more of Him.

Do you think you are ready to decrease so His character can increase in your life? I hope so! Are you prepared to die to your selfish ambitions and ego? If the answer is yes, then you need to know that there must be a readiness within you—a readiness to pick up your cross and to die daily, like Jesus said.

There is no other way to become Christ-like and for God to receive all the glory. Paul said that he would glory only in the cross of our Lord Jesus Christ, "by whom the world is crucified unto me, and I unto the world." (Galatians 6:14) To put it into my own words, Paul is saying, "I am dead to the world and the world is dead to me. So now if you decrease, His fruit (character) will increase in you."

"And he said to them all, 'If any man will come after me, let him deny himself, and take up his cross daily, and follow me. For whosoever will save his life shall lose it: but whosoever will lose his life for my sake, the same shall save it'".
Luke 9:23-24

Each fruit of the Spirit is an empowering force that was infused into every born-again person's spirit at salvation. The "fruit" that is in the spirit of each believer will manifest only when he or she learns to yield to it during spiritual attacks and opposition.

Our enemy, Satan, opposes us every step of the way when we make a move toward God. This is because he doesn't want us to be salt or light in the world and he wants to see us fail miserably. So, his plan is to confront us with temptation in the arena of the nine fruits of the Spirit, which I also like to call the "Nine Spiritual Fronts". I will cover each Spiritual Front in the following chapters to give you some understanding of each.

Here is a small example of what I am speaking about: If you are tempted with the thought of holding onto bitterness and are struggling to forgive someone, then you are at the Love Front. If you are being tempted to abuse drugs you are at the Self-Control Front. Satan's main objective is to wear you out to the point that you will want to give up. He wants to discourage you in your walk with God. The word *discouragement* comes from a French word that means to "cut the heart out"[1]. Satan wants to cut out your heart; he wants to disempower you by assassinating your character. The Holy Spirit, however, wants to encourage you or put your heart back in and enlarge it so you can be the godly man or woman He has called you to be.

The Apostle John lets us in on the battle plan of Satan in his epistle:

"The thief's purpose is to steal and kill and destroy…"
John 10:10a (NLT)

Then, Jesus reveals His battle plan and notice that it is the complete opposite of Satan's plan:

---

1   *Heath's French and English Dictionary*, compiled by James Boïelle, James Bertrand de Vincheles Payen-Payne, published by D. C. Heath, 1903

"…My purpose is to give them a rich and satisfying life."
John 10:10b (NLT)

This is why we must bear, on purpose, the fruit of the Spirit. Bearing fruit is God's agenda, and the works of the flesh are Satan's agenda. We either yield to the flesh or we yield to the Spirit. It is our choice, yet be encouraged and know this—we will always outlast the schemes the devil tries to use against us. There is nothing that can stop us when we are aligned with the character of Christ. We will fulfill our assignment here on earth and God will receive all the glory.

I once heard this statement: "Ministry emerges from personal character."

Listen, you may be in the ministry, but if you lack the character of God, you'll lack effective ministry. Sure, you may be as sharp as a knife concerning the ins and outs of the ministry. You may be a genius in the administration area, a whizz at social media, and you may even preach a masterpiece once in a while. But the words you speak will not leave a lasting impression upon the hearts of your listeners. Why? Because your words will not carry the weight of His anointing, and they will not pierce the hearts of your listeners, due to your lack of character. Matthew wrote:

"When Jesus had finished saying these things, the crowds were amazed at his teaching, for he taught with real

authority—quite unlike their teachers of religious law."
Matthew 7:28-29 (NLT)

As your character develops, the words you speak will carry His authority and anointing:

"If any man speaks let him speak as the oracles of God..."
1 Peter 4:11a

If you want your words to pierce the hearts of your listeners, then allow me to put forth a challenge to you. Along with reading the Bible and praying, read this book and do the devotions at the end of each chapter. More importantly, make an inward decision to walk like Jesus did on this earth. I also recommend that you find someone you trust who will help keep you accountable. Please, concerning those who keep you accountable, always remember that it is an honor and a privilege for someone to have that kind of influence in your life.

Let's imagine for a moment that you are at the threshold of a whole new life, a life of ongoing breakthroughs in your prayers, doors of opportunity suddenly flinging open, new relationships coming into your life that will thrust you forward in your assignment and your destiny. May you come to realize, as I have, that this is something better to be found than gold, as the Word tells us:

"My fruit is better than gold, yea, than fine gold..."
Proverbs 8:19a

CHAPTER ONE

THE MALFUNCTION

IN TODAY'S world, watching the news or reading the local newspaper can cause a rise in anyone's anxiety level. Whether it's news of another drive-by shooting that claimed the life of one of our young people, or the threat of a nuclear war—one story after another like these would unnerve anyone.

Please know that you're not alone in this and most people are bewildered in trying to understand the psyche of this world. Current events like this can stir up questions like: Was it always like this? Has humanity gone completely helter-skelter? Is the world going to get worse or will this madness ever go away? All very good questions, but maybe those are the wrong questions to ask. Why not ask, "Is there a solution to the world's problems?"

Having a solution is defined by the act of solving problems. Now, anyone can find a problem these days, but not everyone can find a solution to the problem. Right off the bat, I want you to know that I do not have the solution to the world's problems! I can, however, give you a hint of Who does have the solution by sharing a line from one of my favorite Gospel songs, by Andraé Crouch: *"Jesus is the answer for the world today, above Him there's no other, Jesus is the way."* [2]

The earth was originally created with a beauty, a freshness, a purity and with a divine order of the peace of God surrounding everything and everyone. God did not create the world in the condition that it is in now. This condition of this world is directly related to condition of the hearts of people and the decisions that flow from their hearts.

IN THE BIBLE

It is from reading the Bible that even a casual reader could come to the simple conclusion that something has gone terribly wrong. The first three chapters of Genesis help us see the distinction between where mankind began and where we are now.

---

2 *Jesus is the Answer*, by Andraé & Sandra Crouch, ©1973 Bud John Songs, Inc. (Admin Song Solutions)

Adam and Eve, the first man and woman, were created and put in Paradise. One can but scratch their head thinking about how the God-breathed perfect man and perfect woman, who were living the perfect life in a perfect world, who had a perfect relationship given to them by the perfect God, could just go out and blow it away and lose everything they had.

How good did Adam and Eve really have it, one may ask? Well, Genesis 1:31a says:

> *"And God saw every thing that he had made, and, behold, it was very good…"*

So, we see that mankind was created "very good", or should I say the "God kind of good". Other than that, we are left to use our imaginations to envision how good life was for them. The first man and woman enjoyed the "God kind of life"—no worries, no cares and never a thought of fear or anxiety. They were blessed with perfect health every day of their lives.

This all changed on one of those "normal" God kind of days. On that day, the spiritual atmosphere shifted and a different presence was ushered in by an intruder, a trespasser who arrived on the scene. It's interesting to me that Adam and Eve didn't seem to be frightened or alarmed by it. The presence of this creature must have been familiar to them, but something was different.

This creature positioned itself on the path they were

walking and began to communicate with them. Now, of course, we, knowing the story, are very much aware that this was the "thief in the night" whose intentions were to steal, kill and destroy Adam and Eve. He used a weapon that was so powerful that even today we must remain vigilant lest we ourselves also fall from grace. That weapon was *deception.* The enemy was very good at using this tactic, for he was the Father of Deception (lies). Let's zoom in on what happened.

Genesis 3:1-7 (NLT) says:

"The serpent was the shrewdest of all the wild animals the LORD God had made. One day he asked the woman, "Did God really say you must not eat the fruit from any of the trees in the garden?" "Of course we may eat fruit from the trees in the garden," the woman replied. "It's only the fruit from the tree in the middle of the garden that we are not allowed to eat. God said, 'You must not eat it or even touch it; if you do, you will die.'" "You won't die!" the serpent replied to the woman. "God knows that your eyes will be opened as soon as you eat it, and you will be like God, knowing both good and evil." The woman was convinced. She saw that the tree was beautiful and its fruit looked delicious, and she wanted the wisdom it would give her. So she took some of the fruit and ate it. Then she gave some to her husband, who was with her, and he ate it, too. At that moment their eyes were opened, and they suddenly felt shame at

their nakedness. So they sewed fig leaves together to cover themselves."

MALFUNCTION: CAUSED BY SIN

Look at that: all of a sudden the man and the woman found themselves naked and ashamed! That's interesting because the Bible says that the man and his wife were both naked originally, but they felt no shame. (Genesis 2:25) So why, after living their whole lives in the presence of God had they never noticed that they were naked? Why was it suddenly an issue? One moment, they were walking around naked and carefree, and the next moment they were ashamed of their nakedness.

How ashamed where they? They were ashamed enough that they reached for the leaves of the closest tree and tied them around their bodies and then hid behind some bushes! At the snap of a finger Adam and Eve's perception of themselves and of their relationship to God changed. There was a shift. Something—everything—was different to them. This is what I refer to as 'The Malfunction'. The dictionary defines *malfunction* as "the failure to function properly."[3]

So, when Adam and Eve chose to listen to the creature and to disobey God, it was as if they had thrown a monkey wrench into the gears of the order of creation.

But nothing surprises our God! He only has Plan A. There is never a Plan B, so nothing surprised Him—

---

3   https://www.dictionary.com/browse/malfunction

not even this virus that had entered into the creation plan and had caused a massive disruption in His original prototype design for the human being, which was "fearfully and wonderfully made" in the image of the Almighty God. (Psalm 139:24)

THE EVE OF THE WORKS OF THE FLESH

The disobedience of Adam and Eve eventually caused them to be found standing naked and exposed. God's command was clear: "Do not eat the forbidden fruit." So, because of their disobedience to God, Adam and Eve found themselves naked and in the flesh. They went from "good naked" to "bad naked". Their sin of disobedience birthed the works of the flesh. (Humorously, one could say that Adam and Eve were the founders of the First Church of the Fig Leaf!) Self-righteousness was also birthed and the battle between the Spirit and the works of the flesh began to ensue.

Adam and Eve went from having a beautiful, spiritual experience with God to having a dreaded human experience apart from God. It is important to keep this in mind, believer—we are not godless human beings seeking a spiritual experience, but rather we are spiritual beings and, with God, we can live and have a victorious human experience.

When Adam and Eve chose to eat the Forbidden Fruit, it was like the fangs of the serpent had penetrated the flesh of humanity and its evil venom had rushed through the veins of mankind. Just as quickly, the God-breathed spirit of life that had been inside of Adam and Eve left, and their spirits were stricken dead with the adversary's DNA. God had to cast them out of Paradise and into a world that had also become infected with sin and chaos. We can still see the realities of this malicious malfunction in our world today.

I have always enjoyed the following statement because it is so true and I have definitely experienced it for myself:

Sin will take you further than you want to go;
Keep you longer than you want to stay;
Cost you more than you want to pay.[4]

Since the fall in the Garden, mankind has been abused by sin and it has put us all into dire straits. We would have been wiped off the face of this planet if it were not for the fulfillment of the promise of our gracious God in Genesis 3:15, regarding the birth of the Messiah, Jesus our Lord.

Salvation would have been only a thought if it hadn't been for the mercy of God. Still, for thousands of years, mankind has been involved with the works of the flesh and they are wearing us out. This is why we must come to Jesus. Can you now see the strength of this Scripture?

---

4   Source unknown

"Then Jesus said, "Come to me, all of you who are weary and carry heavy burdens, and I will give you rest. Take my yoke upon you. Let me teach you, because I am humble and gentle at heart, and you will find rest for your souls. For my yoke is easy to bear, and the burden I give you is light."
Matthew 11:28-30 (NLT)

THE DEVICE

We will always have choices in our lives that will lead us into either the 'Higher Life' or the 'Lower Life'. There was an element that God put into the "perfect prototypes", Adam and Eve, that amazes me to no end. One may think, "Is it to blame? Was this the reason for the malfunction? Is the Creator to blame? Do we have a case for a lawsuit?" Well, I doubt it very much.

That's because what our Creator put in us, He also put us in charge of. That element is called Free Will. The dictionary defines *free will* as the "power of acting without the constraint of necessity or fate; the ability to act at one's own discretion."[5]

We have been given the ability, along with the responsibility, to choose either the Higher Life or the Lower Life. The consequences of our decision unfold when we choose, or refuse, to enter into a fruitful relationship with Jesus. Saint, if you have made some

---

5   https://www.dictionary.com/browse/free-will

very bad choices in your life, like the rest of us, then please be assured of this: Jesus *can* fix it! Oh yes, He can—He did for me several times in my life. Of course, I cannot guarantee that everything will go back to your "normal", but if you will trust Him, you can believe for a new normal. No one can promise that you will win the lottery and everything will be hunky-dory. I will say this to you: God can make a difference in your life and He—and only He—can restore the years that sin has eaten away.

Jesus is calling *you*. He is calling you to the 'Higher Life' through a relationship with Him—the uplifted life, the better life, the life of empowerment, the abundant life.

Listen, Christianity is not about a bunch of rules and regulations. Christianity is about empowerment! God takes us mere humans and empowers us to live a life that pleases Him as we yield to Him! It is empowerment by relationship. His power will transform you. The works of the flesh, on the other hand, will abuse you.

SPEAKING OF RELATIONSHIPS...

The Holy Spirit spoke to me one day through my good friend Andy Elmes, senior pastor of Family Church in the UK, while I was attending a leadership meeting with my local team. Andy made a statement that resonated in my spirit. He said, "Learn to celebrate relationships." That one statement birthed another in me: "Christianity is all about relationships." Think about it—no person can enter heaven without a relationship with Jesus Christ.

"Jesus saith unto him, I am the way, the truth, and the life: no man cometh unto the Father, but by me."
John 14:6

With careful, focused study of the Scriptures, one will come to the realization of how much God values relationships. It is revealed in His command, as written by John:

"A new commandment I give unto you, that ye love one another; as I have loved you, that ye also love one another. By this shall all men know that ye are my disciples, if ye have love one to another."
John 13:34-35

In the Old Testament, God gives us the Ten Commandments and because of His holiness God observes us as we encounter our weakness and our struggles in the flesh. With the grace of the New Testament, we see that Jesus gave just one commandment: "Love one another." Then He comes into our spirits and empowers us to obey that commandment—just like the prophecy of Ezekiel when he wrote:

"And I will put my spirit within you, and cause you to walk in my statutes, and ye shall keep my judgments, and do them."
Ezekiel 36:27

God created us with the ability to have relationships and to maintain them. That, my friend, will take a concentrated effort in bearing the fruits of the Spirit in your life, your marriage, your home and ministry.

The word *concentrated* means to 'apply with all one's attention and energy."[6] The word *effort* means "the exertion of physical or mental power, or an earnest and strenuous attempt for achievement."[7]

God gave us the various fruits of the Spirit to help us have and maintain healthy relationships. Can you see how much God desires our relationships to be fruitful?

"But Brother Danny, you have no idea what is going on in my life. My spouse, my children and my home are in chaos. How can I get them to line up with what I am trying to do?" Well first, before I answer, let me share the following with you:

A flight attendant, during the safety talk before a flight, says, "If the air pressure in the cabin drops, oxygen masks will fall down in front of you." Then she says the most important point: "Put your *own* mask on first before helping anyone else."

---

6   https://www.dictionary.com/browse/concentrated

7   https://www.dictionary.com/browse/effort

That's an excellent teaching principle. Take care of yourself *first* in regards to *your* walk with God, and then you will be able to help others. Bring forth the fruit of the Spirit in your life and watch your relationships become enriched—in your marriage, family, children, friends and even in business and ministerial relationships. Also keep this in mind—healthy relationships tend to open the doors of opportunity. I cannot emphasis that strongly enough.

Allow me to prophesy over you: *God will shut some relational doors that have hindered you and will open doors that will position you in fruitful relationships for fruitful endeavors.*

Our destinies are connected to our relationships so we must value them. Allow your heart to be fixed and make up your mind to bring forth fruit.

The Scripture declares, "By this (love) shall all men know that you are my disciples, if you have love one to another." (John 13:35) If the works of the flesh are manifesting in your life on a regular, consistent basis, they will hinder your relationships in a big, big way.

I think this is a good place to remind you of this again:

Sin will take you farther that you want to go
Keep you longer than you want to stay
Cost you more than you want to pay

Listen, if you are a young Christian, be determined to bear fruit. Memorize Galatians 5:22, study the fruits of the Spirit and work to bear them in your life. Keep in mind the old saying, "Character goes before Charisma (gifting)."

The following phrase is mentioned seven times in the book of Revelations, "He that has ears to hear; let him hear what the Spirit is saying to the Church."

So, hear and fear (reverence, awe) God.

FOR PERSONAL REFLECTION OR DISCUSSION

• Have you found it difficult to maintain healthy relationships?

• Do you feel it was always the other party's fault?

• Could you have played a part in some of the broken relationships?

• Do you believe that the fruit of the Spirit will help you build relationships? Why?

• What should we value in our everyday lives?

• Have you ever hated someone before?

• Have you forgiven them?

• If not, are you willing to forgive them now?

LET'S PRAY

Pray this prayer to prepare the way for the Holy Spirit's character to be released within you:

Heavenly Father, I pray in the name of Jesus that You strengthen my commitment to You and ask for help so I can bear the fruit of Your Son's character. I have no excuse now, I understand what I must do and I am ready to yield wholeheartedly and passionately to your Spirit. I anticipate that my life will bring in a harvest that pleases You. Lord, please help me to value my relationships for I know my destiny is connected to them.

Amen.

CHAPTER TWO

THE YOU FACTOR: ALTER EGO

LET'S TALK ABOUT THE REAL YOU

WHILE WATCHING a cop show one day, a character made a comment that intrigued me. He said, "Evil people do evil things; good people do stupid things." That statement may not be an absolute truth, but it did cause me to reflect. We are all human and I am sure that you, like myself, have entered the 'Stupid Zone' more than once. Yet. While many concentrate on what you did, it would be more productive and beneficial to think about why you did it.

For myself, it was an eye opener when I discovered the 'why' behind what I was doing. God used it to reveal to me where I was in my walk with Him. It also created an urgency to develop a plan for my life that would stop the negative behavior. Hopefully this chapter will help you discover the same and give you an advantage in overcoming those weak moments that might lead you into the 'Stupid Zone'.

The spiritual warfare we face every day is that of our sinful flesh pushing us to do just the opposite of what the Spirit wants. These two forces battle for the right-of-way into our hearts and minds.

Let's read what the Apostle Paul wrote:

> "…These two forces are constantly fighting each other, so you are not free to carry out your good intentions. But when you are directed by the Spirit, you are not under obligation to the law of Moses."
> **Galatians 5:17b-18 (NLT)**

In other words, you are free to choose.

To this day, I am drawn to teachings concerning the Holy Spirit with regards to hearing and listening for direction for my life, so please bear with me as I share the following slightly silly story with an important message:

A young man became keenly aware early in his life of his own Guardian Angel. Every day he would scan his surroundings hoping to spot his angel, and when he did he would shoot his angel an affirming smile.

On the day of his high school graduation, the young man graduated at top of the class so his parents, being proud and grateful for what their son had achieved, gifted him with a new, red sports car. As they threw him the keys they said, "Drive safely!" The young man snatched the keys in mid-air and responded with a prudent, "Absolutely, Mom and Dad!"

He enjoyed his gift immensely. One day, as the young man was out driving, he noticed that his Guardian Angel was sitting atop his new car. The angel was smiling, with his legs crossed and hair blowing back with the wind. This became the norm for them after that day, for both the angel and the young man enjoyed riding with each other and sharing each other's company.

Several weeks later, the young man decided to see how fast his car could go. He entered the ramp onto the highway and began to gently press down on the accelerator. As he watched the speedometer rise to 35-40 mph, the young man glanced up to see his Guarding Angel joyfully sitting on the roof. Soon he was traveling at 40-50 mph and the Angel was still on the roof. Then he got up to 50-60 mph, yet the angel was still on the roof. The young man pressed down further harder on the accelerator, getting to 70, then 80-85 mph. As he reached 90 mph, the young man glanced up quickly and realized that his Guardian Angel was no longer there.

Anxiety began rise up in his stomach as he heard a police siren and, looking in the rear-view mirror, he noticed the flashing lights of a motorcycle policeman. And guess who was riding on the back of the motorcycle, pointing his finger towards the sports car so the police officer would take notice? That's right, his Guardian Angel. Haha!

This humorous, fictitious, story about an angel showed me two valuable points in regards to my relationship with the Holy Spirit. First, we must not grieve the Holy Spirit, and second, we are in the place of His grace when we are following the leading of the Holy Spirit.

Surely you desire the favor of God in your life? Then I suggest you train yourself to be sensitive to the Holy Spirit. That training is necessary in enabling us to walk the straight path of the Spirit. You know, one would think that most Christians would have a sincere desire to be a vessel of honor, fit for the Master's use. Some do not, however, for many unknown reasons, while others believe it is only for a select few. That is an incorrect interpretation of Scripture. Let's read what Paul wrote to Timothy:

> *"But in a great house there are not only vessels of gold and of silver, but also of wood and of earth; and some to honor, and some to dishonor."*
> *2 Timothy 2:20*

Some would stop there and reason within themselves. Some who are not taught in righteousness can live in condemnation and limit themselves by it. They would eliminate themselves as being an honored vessel. Some may say, "Oh, I am not worthy to be used by God. I'm not intelligent, good looking, old enough or young enough." Yet, the Holy Spirit isn't through speaking on the subject, so let's read the very next verse:

"If a man therefore purge (cleanse himself) from these, he shall be a vessel unto honor, sanctified, and meet for the master's use, and prepared unto every good work."
2 Timothy 2:21 (clarification mine)

Do you see that? "If a man therefore purge himself...", or, in other words, if you keep yourself pure. This is a free will privilege, it's a choice. The word *purge* in the Greek means to "cleanse thoroughly"[8]. If you've ever had a colonoscopy (don't you love them?) you will relate to this because the day before the procedure doctors will give you a prescription to help you clean out or cleanse your body so they can conduct a more thorough examination. Yes, it is gross, but that is what iniquity is in the eyes of God: "gross darkness".

Please know that this doesn't refer to perfection. No one is perfect, yet God is pleased when someone is committed to their own personal sanctification and to

---

8   Strong's reference: 2508, *kathairó*

learning to walk in righteousness. God has always used imperfect people to preach His perfect message, so it is important to apply grace to yourself. Yet, that doesn't mean you should allow a spirit of compromise into your life.

THE SPIRIT OF COMPROMISE

Have you met Mr. Gray yet? He will come knocking on your door several times in your life. Most assuredly you will find him at the forks in the road of your life. These 'forks' are the moments of important decisions in our lives. Those moments when we have to choose to be true to God or to compromise the trust people have put in us. Not all compromise is bad. There are times where it is a necessity, such as in the arena of marriage (or your marriage won't blossom!). *Compromise*, in the dictionary, means "to weaken (a reputation or principle) by accepting standards that are lower than is desirable."[9] You can compromise your character by endangering your godly reputation. When you stand strong on the Word of God, it will help clear up any confusion. Drawing a line of demarcation between black and white, between right and wrong, doesn't really leave much room for Mr. Gray.

We are either walking in the Spirit or walking according to the flesh. One is carnal, the other is spiritual. To overcome compromise, you have to "gird up the loins of

---

9   https://en.oxforddictionaries.com/definition/compromise

your mind" before you come to the next crossroads of your life. Then, then the decision making may be a little easier.

Speaking of crossroads, my lovely bride Jean Marie and I enjoy traveling together, especially driving. Often, when we come to a crossroad on a highway, things may sometimes get a little challenging, even confusing and contentious in our car. We each have our own opinion on the correct or quickest way to go. (I believe the invention of the GPS has saved my marriage!) My point in sharing this is that no one is perfect and we are all growing in God, but there are moments in our lives when our fleshly minds make a detour from the way of the Spirit, which causes confusion and contention in our lives and in the lives of those around us. Now, this brings me to the second part.

THE OTHER YOU

Let's talk about the 'Other You' now. What is your initial reaction when you hear about someone doing something that is completely contrary to who they are or how you know them to be? You may hear folks say, "He behaved totally out of character." How about an example closer to home? Do you have children? Have they ever totally embarrassed you by acting out at the grocery store? You give them 'the look' which means, "I am going to take care of you when we get home". Boy, I got that a lot. Still do, occasionally!

Moving on, how about you? Have you ever done or

said something you were embarrassed about? Did words shoot out of your mouth that you later had to apologize for? I am not sure if this is any consolation to you, but be at peace, you are not alone.

There's even a psychological term for the above behavior—it's called *acting out.*

The dictionary definition of *acting out* is "a (usually irritating) impulsive and seemly uncontrollable outburst by a problem child or, what they call, a neurotic adult."[10] Acting out is a defense mechanism that causes us to react when the pressures of life seem overwhelming.

One could say that acting out is our way of escape, or that it is our pressure release valve during times of life's pressures, when we do not know how to or don't want to deal with it.

This brings us to the title of this chapter: *Alter Ego.*

Alter ego is a Latin phrase that means "the other I" or "a sub-conscious in a second self, which is believed to be distinct from a person's normal or original personality."[11] Someone who has an alter ego is one who leads a double life.

Wow, what a definition! Let's look at that again: *A person who has an alter ego is one who leads a double life.* Before I go further, I'd like to clarify my thoughts on this topic. I would suggest that your alter ego is essentially a character flaw in your life. I am not so much speaking

---

10 https://www.merriam-webster.com/dictionary/acting%20out

11 https://www.merriam-webster.com/dictionary/alter%20ego

about funny, celebrity alter egos, such as The Fresh Prince/Will Smith, Hannah Montana/Miley Cyrus, Marky Mark/Mark Wahlburg, Pee Wee Herman/Paul Reuben, Geraldine Jones/Flip Wilson, or Jimmy Glick/Martin Short. Most of these have made a living playing someone else, with many people never knowing who the real person is.

Concerning us, however, there will be situations, scenarios and circumstances that you and I will face in the future, which will challenge us to our very limits. These may bring us to a place of fierce trial and temptation and if we are not strong in the Lord and in the power of His might, we may buckle under the stress and act out.

Allow me to pause here and share with you what I believe is the right way to respond to fierce trials and temptations.

> *"The temptations in your life are no different from what others experience. And God is faithful. He will not allow the temptation to be more than you can stand. When you are tempted, he will show you a way out so that you can endure."*
> *1 Corinthians 10:13 (NLT)*

When we act out the wrong way, we may do a variety of different things. We may begin to use vulgar language, or have an outburst of anger, or storm out of the room and slam the door while leaving an issue unsettled and seemingly forgotten (at least until we act out again). Others act out by using manipulation and emotionally shutting down, or cutting off relationships, or even giving others the silent treatment. Unfortunately, some will act out using violence in one form or another. Others may resort to name calling and causing harmful, emotional damage to their long-term relationships, leaving a loved one deeply wounded.

There are some natural ways to help release the pressure in your life, called "Stress Releasers". Some people like going to a day spa to get a massage or a facial. Others stay at home and take a hot bubble bath with lighted candles, while some may indulge with chocolate-covered strawberries, or even a pot of tea. And there are those who train themselves to remain calm or even count to ten.

All of these are all good in and of themselves—they are simply natural ways to release stress. But there are spiritual ways that are far more powerful: stay in the Word; meditate on a Scripture that God has given you in the past or a prophecy that was spoken to you; soak in His presence with songs of worship; pray aloud with thanksgiving and praise for God for all He has done; journal all the things He has done for you. Oh! If we would only labor to enter into His rest (Hebrews 4:11a).

My lovely bride, Jean Marie, and I took what is called the Harrison Behavior Assessment. This is what corporations use to gather info on potential new employees. It helps them assess individuals and get a glimpse into the possibility of how compatible they may be with their new employers before being hired. This was an eye-opener for us because it revealed two important things. First, it revealed that we are truly soul mates—every area where I was weak, she was strong and every area she was weak, I was strong. We are a good balance. God is a good matchmaker, isn't He? Second, we discovered that certain situations and circumstances in our lives could very well present challenges for us and create stress and pressure. We saw some highlighted areas on the paper, and the consultant said that these were our 'stress points' or, as she called them, "possible tornadoes". 'Tornadoes' are those times when we feel we are backed into a corner with seemingly no way of escape, and if we do not learn how to manage that stress we will act out in some way.

This is where I realized something, and it gave me the idea for the title of this chapter. When we act out from one of these stress points, when we enter into a tornado, we enter the flesh realm. We act out and our alter ego manifests. (By the way, I have five stress points, so don't mess with me! Haha!)

Alter ego is also used to refer to the different behaviors any person may display in certain situations. There are some neurotic people who will live out an alter ego to the maximum, in that they literally lose themselves in that alter ego. Some are pathological liars, serial killers, manipulators and imposters, to name a few.

The biographical book *Catch Me If You Can* tells the story of the life of Frank Abagnale who, before his nineteenth birthday, had successfully pulled off schemes and cons worth millions of dollars by posing as a Pan American World Airways pilot, a Georgia doctor, and a Louisiana parish prosecutor. This young man had issues, but the good news is that Frank Abagnale, after serving his time, was then hired by the FBI to help them understand and solve fraud cases.[12]

Another real-life alter ego story is that of William Queen. Back in 1998, veteran law enforcement agent Queen was given the opportunity go undercover inside the San Fernando chapter of the Mongols, an outlaw motorcycle club and confirmed organized crime syndicate. He became what the Mongols called a 'prospect'—the entry level for anyone who wanted to join the club. Their job description was simple: do whatever anyone in the club tells you to do all the time, or get the snot beaten out of you. Some commands were fairly simple and low key, like shining members' boots or motorcycle, or fetching them a beer. After some time of showing himself worthy, William was inducted into full membership. In his book *Under and Alone* Queen wrote that when he received his membership patch he raised it up, shouting out loud, "I'm a Mongol, I'm a Mongol!"

---

12 Frank Abagnale & Stan Redding, *Catch Me If You Can: The True Story Of A Real Fake*, 2011 Random House

while inside his head he was saying, "I'm a cop, a cop . . . Oh my God, who am I?" He admitted in his book that he almost lost himself.[13]

Christians can be prone to the same experience. How, you may ask? Well, we tend to lose ourselves by forgetting who we are and who we belong to, and we forget about the power and authority that Christ has given to us.

Why? Well, because when we walk in the works of the flesh, in which we have behaved so badly for so long, we begin to feel unworthy and unfit for the promises of God. Let me quickly say this about your acting out: *It is not who you are!* The real you doesn't desire to do wrong, it's your flesh that is acting out.

What you have to learn is to separate your alter ego (fleshly behavior) from the real you. You are a child of God. You're washed by the blood of the Lamb and your name is written in the Lamb's Book of Life. Oh, sure, we are still responsible for our actions and we must own up to them, but please do not claim that these actions define who you are—that's a lie that Satan wants you to believe.

Look at what Paul wrote:

"And those who belong to Christ Jesus (the Messiah) have crucified the flesh (the godless human nature) with

---

13 William Queen, *Under and Alone: Infiltrating the World's Most Violent Motorcycle Gang,* 2005 Penguin Random House LLC

its passions and appetites and desires."
Galatians 5:24 (AMPC)

Now getting back to our alter egos. We don't make big, obvious changes. We don't go out and change out of what we are wearing into some kind of costume, or put on a wig or change our names and then start to rap, sing or dance. Instead, this is what we do: we put a mask over our real selves, a mask of our fleshly attitude and behavior that is contrary to what God has created us to be. When we do that we become the other 'I', our alter ego.

"So, I say, let the Holy Spirit guide your lives. Then you won't be doing what your sinful nature (flesh) craves."
Galatians 5:16 (NLT, clarification mine)

This is so very important to remember, so pay attention to these next few words. When you are born again God doesn't empower *your* character, He empowers you with *His* character. Now, go ahead read it again. Write it down or even memorize it. That is massive, saint!

In closing this chapter, I am going to share a story with you that I heard from the pulpit when I was a young saint. It was spoken not by my Pastor, but by another preacher on staff and because I was young in the Lord, I accepted it as a spiritual truth. (Please keep in mind that, even though this sounds good, it is biblically incorrect!) The story goes like this:

There was a young Native American brave who approached a legendary, wise, old chief. The young brave told the chief about his personal struggles as a young man saying, "It seems that I have two dogs living inside of me, a white dog and a black dog. When the white dog is in the forefront I do good things, but when the black dog is in the forefront I do bad things. I am so confused and I do not know what to do." There was a long silent pause mixed with anticipation and then the wise, legendary chief responded with his wisdom: "Starve the dog you don't want!"[14]

I can see the concept and reasoning behind this, but I will tell you what I see as an error in this teaching, one which often seeps into the believer's mind. The Bible teaches that when we are born again, our old, sinful, human spirit becomes a new, clean, righteous creature. We do not "turn over a new leaf", we become a whole new creation.

Paul says:

"Therefore if any man be in Christ, he is a new creature: old things are passed away; behold, all things are become new."
2 Corinthians 5:17

---

14 In researching this story I found that its origin is only tenuously associated with Native American folklore, but that most people who have heard it, have heard it in that context. I have no wish to offend any readers of Native American ethnicity or association in giving it that context, and I hope I haven't caused any offence.

As a born-again Christian, you do *not* have any black and white dogs living in you. The One you have living in you now is the Spirit of Christ, the Son of the Living God. What must die is our flesh and our fleshly behavior because, as you know, the biggest struggle that you and I will ever have on this planet is our flesh. Now, you'll be able to see the strength of this Scripture:

> *"Watch ye and pray, lest ye enter into temptation. The spirit truly is ready, but the flesh is weak."*
> **Mark 14:38**

See that? Our born-again spirit is always ready, it is always pulsating with life, it is regenerating and the Spirit is always willing and ready for us to tap in by simply yielding to Him. Go ahead, yield and grow.

I wanted to share something that transpired while Jean Marie and I were being evaluated by our Harrison Behavior consultant. She noticed that I have five stress points or, as she called them, "tornadoes". She looked up at me and said, "Wow, you have five tornadoes, you must blow up a lot?!" My wife interjected, "No he doesn't." The consultant looked back at the survey and replied, "Oh yes, I see here that you know how to manage your stress."

The bigger question is—do you?

FOR PERSONAL REFLECTION/DISCUSSION

- What do you think about the Scripture in 1 John 3:8b

which says, "For this purpose the Son of God was manifested, that He might destroy the works of the devil"?

- Do you have a Black Dog and a White Dog in you?
- Do you have several stress points?
- What do you do to manage your stress points?

LET'S PRAY

Pray this prayer to prepare the way for the Holy Spirit's character to be released within you:

Lord, that is exactly what I want You to be to me: Lord! The Lord of my life. I ask you, Jesus, to help me walk like You walked, for I know that the Spirit that empowered Your life was made available to me when I was born again. I will mortify the works of my flesh. I reckon my flesh dead and buried with Jesus, and the life that I now live in the flesh, I live by the faith of the Son of God, who loved me and gave His life for me.
Amen.

CHAPTER THREE

LOVE: THE MAIN INGREDIENT

LET'S IMAGINE for a moment that there is a label on the forehead of every person you meet, a label similar to the U.S. government's nutritional label that is on any kind of food packaging. This label would enable anyone to walk up to us and read what we are full of. That is a very interesting concept, isn't it?

According to consumer laws, manufacturers must list product ingredients in descending order of predominance by weight. This means that the ingredient that weighs the most in the product is listed first, and the ingredient that weighs the least is listed last. For example, if you look at the label on the can of a Diet Pepsi you'll notice that the main ingredient of the product is carbonate.

Let's take a look at the ingredients that are supposed to be in every born-again Christian:

> *"But the fruit of the Spirit is love, joy, peace, long-suffering, gentleness, goodness, faith, meekness, temperance…"*
> **Galatians 5:22-23a**

I suppose our "Person Label" could look something like this:

Love

Joy

Peace

Long-suffering (Patience)

Gentleness

Goodness

Faith

Meekness (Humility)

Temperance (Self-control)

First of all, please know that I am not diminishing any fruit of the Spirit by placing it at the bottom of the list. I am simply using this analogy to make a point.

Why is *love* listed first in this Scripture? Would *love* be listed first because it is the most important out of all the fruit of the Spirit? I am going to stick my neck out and say, "Yes!" My reasoning for this is based on what the Apostle John said:

> *"By this shall all men know that ye are my disciples, if ye have love one to another."*
> **John 13:35**

Take notice that John did not say, "Because you have great self-control and you have mastered many things". Or, "Because you speak in tongues and carry a Bible all the time". Neither, "Because you go to church regularly and say 'Praise the Lord' and 'Thank you, Jesus'." No, John doesn't say that, but rather he says, "They will know that you are a Christian because you *love* one another."

How weighty is love? Well, Paul told the Corinthians:

> *"Three things will last forever—faith, hope, and love—and the greatest of these is love."*
> **1 Corinthians 13:13 (NLT)**

The word *love* is mentioned five times in the letter to the Galatians. Keep in mind that this letter was written specifically so the people of Galatia would experience true freedom from legalism. Paul writes,

> *"For in Jesus Christ neither circumcision availeth any thing, nor uncircumcision; but faith which worketh by love."*
> **Galatians 5:6**

So, as you just read, our faith works by love. The word *worketh*, in the Greek, is *energeó*[15]. This is where we get our English word *energize*, which means to be active and efficient.

So, knowing this, we can rightfully say that our faith is energized when we love with God's love. The Greek word that is used for love in this scripture is *agape*. Agape is different from the English word for love, and the best way for me to describe it is this: human love is limited, agape love is "love without limits".

Agape love is not a feeling, but rather is a deliberate act of one's will to yield to the love of God that He put in us. It is love put into action, which means that we are free to yield to, or reject, the love with which God has empowered us.

I found this great explanation of Agape love on the Compelling Truth website: "Agape love is a sacrificial love that will give us the strength of God, so we can voluntarily suffer inconvenience, discomfort and even death for the benefit of another, without expecting anything in return."[16] In its simpler form, Agape love means, "loving and not expecting anything back." Human love will run out eventually. Human love is limited, but Agape love is unlimited. We believers are not called to love in the way humans love—we are called to love with God's love. It is His love in us and all we have

---

15 Strong's reference: 1754, *energeó*

16 https://www.compellingtruth.org/agape-love.html

to do is yield to what He put in our born-again spirit.

I believe that love is the gateway to the miraculous. The fruits of the Spirit and spiritual gifts are both spiritual and supernatural. One may seem more spectacular than the other. For example, the fruits of the Spirit on the surface may not seem as exciting or as interesting, but the truth of the matter is that the fruits of the Spirit are made up of supernatural forces continually flowing from the re-created spirit of the born-again believer. They allow us the ability to have constant victory in our lives.

Look at what Ephesians, also known as the "power epistle" says:

> *"Therefore be imitators of God, as beloved children. And walk in love, as Christ loved us and gave himself up for us, a fragrant offering and sacrifice to God."*
> **Ephesians 5:1-2 (ESV)**

When you imitate Christ, you are walking in the same love that He did, and you are learning to die to yourself and be a living sacrifice, as He did.

Can you see how important love is? Consider this: *love* is mentioned in the epistle of 1 John forty-six[17] times, all within five short chapters. That's forty-six times—did you get that? Forty-six mentions by the "Apostle of Love".

---

17 In the KJV *love*, or a derivative of the word (loveth, loved), appears forty-six times. I counted!

Here's another one, just for the fun of it. 1 John 4:16 says:

"And we have known and believed the love that God hath to us. God is love; and he that dwelleth in love dwelleth in God, and God in him."

Love is in our spiritual DNA, for God is love. According to Romans 5:1b,

"The love of God is shed abroad in our hearts by the Holy Ghost which is given unto us."

Be assured that I am not saying the other fruits of the Spirit are not equally as important. They are all important when you need them. Trust me, as long as we are living in this world and in this flesh, we must learn to yield to all of the fruit of the Spirit every day. Tests and temptations will always come and will battle with you at these nine Spiritual Fronts, or at the place where the fruit of the Spirit is growing in you. But when we learn to walk in love, it will propel us toward the character of Christ and will help us walk in all of the other fruit. Jesus majored in the fruit of love and the other fruit followed as well.

When a believer matures in their faith and learns to yield to the fruit of love, all the other fruit will surely follow. I think that walking through the door of love will usher us into a spiritual momentum in bearing the fruit of His full character. I love reading the passage below. Please read it slowly and receive the strength of this passage:

> *"Love is patient and kind. Love is not jealous or boastful or proud or rude. It does not demand its own way. It is not irritable, and it keeps no record of being wronged. It does not rejoice about injustice but rejoices whenever the truth wins out. Love never gives up, never loses faith, is always hopeful, and endures through every circumstance."*
> ***1 Corinthians 13:4-7 (NLT)***

The fruit of love will open the floodgates to the growth of all the other fruit. Love creates a flow in your life that will help you overcome anything. Paul says:

> *"Love never fails [it never fades nor ends]…"*
> ***1 Corinthians 13:8a (AMP)***

It's not just *a* choice, it's *your* choice, and when you choose love, you enter the "No Fear Zone"!

> *"There is no fear in love; but perfect love casteth out fear: because fear hath torment. He that feareth is not made perfect in love."*
> ***1 John 4:18***

I would like to point out that the word *perfect* in the Greek means, "completeness or of full age"[18]. That means as we mature in our love we will fundamentally understand that God loves us and that nothing can harm us in any way—fear will have no effect on us.

Makes you want to love somebody now, doesn't it? I posted this on Facebook one day:

Still some may say to God, "Lord, where are the gifts of the Spirit in the Church?" Perhaps God may say, "Where is the fruit of the Spirit in my Church?"

I got remarks like, "Oh, they complement each other, you need both in the church." They couldn't just leave it alone. Quite honestly, I believe the fruits of the Spirit trump spiritual gifts. Love is the greater one.

#CHARACTERGOESBEFORECHARISMA

Do you remember this?

"On judgment day many will say to me, 'Lord! Lord! We prophesied in your name and cast out demons in your name and performed many miracles in your name.' But I will reply, 'I never knew you. Get away from me, you who break God's laws.'"
Matthew 7:22-23 (NLT)

Keep in mind, God commanded us to go and bear fruit, and that our fruit should remain. He never

---

18 Strong's reference: 5048, *teleioó*

commanded us to bear *gifts*, even though we are stewards of them and we must all give an account for our stewardship.

We can choose the "High Life" that God offers us or choose the "Low Life" by refusing to live in love. Remember, it is not just any kind of love, but God's Agape love. I hope you can understand why the Lord gave us the command to love:

> *"A new commandment I give unto you, that ye love one another; I have loved you, that ye also love one another."*
> **John 13:34**

Jesus is saying to His disciples (us) to "love one another". So, our lives are the practice field.

A man once said to me that love is not so much a commandment as something that you just naturally do when you become a Christian. I don't know what planet that person lived on, but definitely not on my planet Earth! Wherever there is human flesh there will be the challenge of character flaws.

Matthew wrote that a man walked up to Jesus one day and asked Him, "Which is the great commandment in the Law?" When I was seeking the Lord in my twenties I was reading the Bible one day and I came across this passage for the very first time. I remember pausing and thinking to myself as I read, "Hmmm, what could be the greatest commandment of God?" I surmised that it had to be, "Thou Shalt not Kill" for sure. Needless to say, I was taken aback when I read Jesus' answer:

> *"Master, which is the great commandment in the law?*
> *Jesus said unto him, Thou shalt love the Lord thy God*
> *with all thy heart, and with all thy soul, and with all*
> *thy mind. This is the first and great commandment.*
> *And the second is like unto it, Thou shalt love thy*
> *neighbor as thyself. On these two commandments hang*
> *all the law and the prophets."*
> **Matthew 22:36-40**

In the Old Testament, God gave mankind Ten Commandments (well, more than that actually), then He seemed to sit back and watch man hopelessly break every single one of them, multiple times.

In the New Testament, Jesus gave us one commandant: That we love one another. He even comes into us by the Holy Spirit and empowers us to obey it. When we are born again, we receive the Person of Love, and our responsibility is to bear that fruit of love, the very nature of God, in our lives.

Responsibility is an awesome word, but I think its meaning is more powerful than it reads. Reversing the compound words brings to light that we have the ability to respond. God has given us the *ability* to have the right *response* to the hate, to the anger, to the hostility that is in this violent world. I believe God holds us responsible with what He has entrusted to us by His precious Holy Spirit.

Listen to what the Holy Spirit has to say to you, thus says the Lord:

> *"Ye have not chosen me, but I have chosen you, and ordained you, that ye should go and bring forth fruit, and that your fruit should remain: that whatsoever ye shall ask of the Father in my name, he may give it you."*
> **John 15:16**

I did not come to God because I loved Him. I came to God because I knew if I died I would go to a devil's hell. Yet, since I have been born again, I keep falling in love with Him over and over again.

> *"We love him, because he first loved us."*
> **1 John 4:19**

As the old song goes: "God is so good; God is so good; God is so good, He's so good to me"[19] (Yes, I sang that out loud and off key!)

Before we can *release* love, we have to *understand* love. Before we can *understand* love, we must *receive* love. When we receive love, then we are obligated to give it

---

19 *God is so good*, Paul Makai (Trans. Marilyn Foulkes)

away, which reminds me of a spiritual law: We only get to keep what we give away. We give love away so easily here in this world. Oh, not the God-kind of love, but a simple, shallow love. We say:

"I love ice cream."

"I love that song."

"I love it when the sun shines."

"I love you, let's have sex."

Yes, we even say this word to manipulate someone into bed. I told my daughters that if a man ever says that to them then it is not real love If someone truly loves you they would honor you by honoring your body. Shallow love isn't really love at all.

Come on, wouldn't you think God's love would run deep? It's broader, longer, deeper than any water and higher than any sky. God's love is unconditional. He loved us before we loved Him. Now that's deep! You want deeper?

"That he would grant you, according to the riches of his glory, to be strengthened with might by his Spirit in the inner man; that Christ may dwell in your hearts by faith; that ye, being rooted and grounded in love, may be able to comprehend with all saints what is the breadth, and length, and depth, and height; and to know the love of Christ, which passeth knowledge, that ye might be filled with all the fulness of God."
Ephesians 3:16-19

Come on, let's go and LOVE our enemies now.

FOR PERSONAL REFLECTION OR DISCUSSION

- Are there people in your life whom you now love that you didn't love before?
- Are there people in your life whom you need to forgive before you love them?
- Is love a choice or does it come naturally when you are saved?
- Are there some DNA traits of your natural, earthly father that you have noticed in your life?
- Whose DNA do you have now and what proves that?
- What is the greatest commandment?
- How's that working for you?

LET'S PRAY

Father, I want to thank You for loving me even before I loved You. You loved me when I didn't give a lick about You. Your love is so amazing to me and I want more of it. I ask You for a baptism of Your love upon my life so I can love like never before. Because of Your love, I do not have to fear, for Your perfect love casts out all fear. Thank You for having my back even when I didn't realize it. You are truly a good, good Father. In Jesus name, thank You; I give myself to you. Amen.

CHAPTER FOUR

RELEASING HIS JOY

SEARCHING FOR gold? I can assure you that it will not be found lying on the ground in little piles waiting to be scooped up! There are only about twenty-two U.S. states where you may have an opportunity to find gold. To discover tremendous amounts of gold you would have to travel to distant lands because the largest known deposits of gold appear on two continents: Africa and India. Of course, keep in mind that there is no guarantee of a strike.

Why is gold so hard to find? Well, gravity is the reason we have to dig deeply because gold is six to seven times heavier than ordinary sediments. So, if you want to discover gold, you will have to labor. You will have to dig. You will have to go deep and you will have to be diligent. At any point in the process you could be just one pick swing away, one shovelful away from the find of your life.

Heaven's gold is far more valuable than earthly gold, but you'll find it in a similar manner—you simply open your heart as you dig deeply into your Bible.

"My fruit is better than gold, yea, than fine gold…"
Proverbs 8:19a

When you find that gold, prepare yourself to release it. As they say: "You only get to keep what you give away." So, let's talk about releasing His joy.

Joy is found in the first cluster of spiritual fruit mentioned earlier—love, joy and peace. The fruit of joy is somewhat unique from the other fruit of the Spirit. I like referring to the joy of the Lord as "God's steroids" or "Kingdom Testosterone". We do not inject ourselves with joy when we need it, we simply yield to it by faith.

The first mention of joy in the Bible is found in Nehemiah 8:10:

"Then he said unto them, Go your way, eat the fat, and drink the sweet, and send portions unto them for whom nothing is prepared: for this day is holy unto our Lord:

neither be ye sorry; for the joy of the Lord is your strength."

This Old Testament passage, in context, is saying that the Lord was pleased with Israel's obedience, and to me, personally, it is saying that God's joy was going to be Israel's strength. This would not have been said if they were disobedient. The New Testament tells us that God doesn't love us according to our obedience or our performance, because Christ performed the ultimate, final sacrifice that brought joy to Himself.

Because of what Christ did, our performance days are (thankfully) over. It's done and all we have to do now is live our lives out of who we are. It's not about doing or performing. It's about *being* and by saying that I mean being "Christ-like".

Joy in the Greek means, "Cheerfulness or a calm delight, or full of cheer"[20]. I would like to point out to you that it is a verb, an action word.

I am not insinuating that we walk around laughing and giggling because that may come across as kind of weird, wouldn't it? And we should be careful not to be like the comic book villain the Joker with his hideous laugh—that would be worse! Joy is cheerfulness or calm delight *deep* within us that God deposited in us at the new birth.

I once worked at a small factory in the Syracuse area

---

20 Strong's reference: 5463, *chairó*

before my full-time ministry opportunity came. The company was called Industrial Fabricating, and I had a boss who got a wrong first impression of me, which caused him to be constantly on my case. It started when I told him that this was the first real job I'd had in two years. I meant that it was the first real job I'd had in two years working for a large company instead of being self-employed, which I had been previously. But in his mind, he thought that I'd been sitting on my bottom doing nothing all during that time. Because of that misunderstanding, my boss pushed me to the limits to try and instill in me a work ethic. (I have to add that it was cleared up on my last day.) He was also a very funny man. That being said, one day I wasn't feeling well and was very tired. I was cutting long sheets of steel about an inch thick into smaller pieces—not a great day and not a great thing to do on a day like that. My foreman walked by, stopped and then came up to me and sheepishly said, "Now don't get me wrong, I do not mean anything about what I am about to say, but you have a really nice smile." Yep, that's what he said, seriously. It was an awkward moment and be assured, he was not hitting on me! But on one of my very worst days, somehow the joy of the Lord noticeably reached all the way up to my face.

Joy was the very thing that kept me going through those rough days with this foreman, who had made it his personal mission to make this Christian miserable.

He even once barked at me and said, "Christians do not make it here."

Now what brings me great joy is that when this very man was dying of a brain tumor, a Christian friend of mine who worked there led him to the Lord. LOL! God is so good, isn't He?

Letting your light shine is always a good thing to do and, quite honestly, it is the will of God for you to do so. Now this next passage helped me get through some difficult times. Let's call it our job description of sorts for how a Christian is supposed to act in public:

> *"Wherefore, my beloved, as ye have always obeyed, not as in my presence only, but now much more in my absence, work out your own salvation with fear and trembling. For it is God which worketh in you both to will and to do of his good pleasure. Do all things without murmurings and disputings: that ye may be blameless and harmless, the sons of God, without rebuke, in the midst of a crooked and perverse nation, among whom ye shine as lights in the world."*
> *Philippians 2:12-15*

Saints, we cannot do this in our own strength, it is simply impossible without God. We are encouraged by the Word and by His Spirit to release what He has given us. Working out our own salvation is simply letting God's character out of us. It's possible for you to do so now because you have His DNA, His creative ability, His Word, His character and His Spirit within you.

We no longer have a sinners' heart, as some preachers preach, but we have God's heart pumping in our redeemed spirit. Ezekiel 36:26-27 says:

> *"A new heart also will I give you, and a new spirit will I put within you: and I will take away the stony heart out of your flesh, and I will give you a heart of flesh. And I will put my spirit within you, and cause you to walk in my statutes, and ye shall keep my judgments, and do them."*

Now the fulfillment of this Scripture is found in 2 Corinthians 5:17-18 (AMPC):

> *"Therefore if any person is [ingrafted] in Christ (the Messiah) he is a new creation (a new creature altogether); the old [previous moral and spiritual condition] has passed away. Behold, the fresh and new has come! But all things are from God, Who through Jesus Christ reconciled us to Himself [received us into favor, brought us into harmony with Himself] and gave to us the ministry of reconciliation [that by word and deed we might aim to bring others into harmony with Him]."*

Proverbs, the book of wisdom, confirms something that I have always felt—that the fruits of the Spirit are the greatest soul-winning tool, ever. The writer of

Proverbs 11:30 (AMPC) says that, "The fruit of the [uncompromisingly] righteous is a tree of life, and he who is wise captures human lives [for God, as a fisher of men—he gathers and receives them for eternity]." KJV says, "…he who *winneth souls* is wise." (emphasis mine)

The fruits of the Spirit activated through us will attract sinners just like insects are attracted to light. We're not "bug zappers", but rather light to a dark world. Unfortunately, some people have zapped others with the works of the flesh thinking that they were doing God justice.

WE KNOW WHY YOU ARE SO HAPPY

I was standing in the kitchen of a single mother's home one time when she said, "You are always happy and we singles were talking about that and we realize why you are filled with happiness." She went on to say, "We came to the conclusion it's because you're married and have children." My first thought was, "Are you flipping kidding me, sister?!"

If you think for one moment that what you have in your life is your source of joy, you are deceived. Your joy source is not your wife, your husband or children. Your source of joy is what God put in you when you were born again. My wife is not responsible for bringing me joy. That is on me.

Now, if you do not have joy in your life it may be

one of these two reasons:

    1) You are not saved;

    2) You gave your joy away.

Keep in mind that *happiness* is not the same as *joy*. This is because happiness is a feeling we have when everything is going our way. A believer has joy whether or not life is going their way. Happiness rides on the back of circumstances; joy rides on the back of God's Word.

Did you ever hear the old gospel song that says, "If the world didn't give it to you then the world can't take it away"? Now, somebody say, "Amen"!

We cannot allow outside stimuli to affect our joy because the joy of the Lord is our strength. If we do not yield to His joy in us we may lose the strength that gets us through that trial, that tribulation, that unfortunate circumstance that we are experiencing.

Now this may not be an accurate psychological assessment, but here are my thoughts: Through personal experience I feel there is a progressive strategy initiated by the enemy that, if not dealt with, can render us powerless in life.

We all have to learn to deal with life's disappointments. That is a fact of life. The progression may go like this: First, disappointment comes and it's like a big, black rain cloud, that hangs over our head. If we do not deal with this disappointment it can break and cascade down upon us, covering us from head to toe with discouragement. Second, when discouragement is not handled with mature thanks and praise to God, and by using our spiritual authority, a spirit of depression has opportunity to capture us and take us as prisoners of war. That is a whole new battle that could rage.

Discouragement is a joy buster. We have to learn to encourage ourselves in the Lord and when we do, our perspective will change. We will move from *our* perspective of the problems we are facing to *God's* perspective. We will go from doubter to believer, from someone who fears to the person of faith we are called to be.

As I said, the spiritual fruit of joy is somewhat unique from the other fruits of the Spirit. That is because the Word says that the joy of the Lord is our *strength.* No other fruit makes that claim. When we encourage ourselves in the Lord, we release God's Kingdom within us, which is righteousness, peace and joy in the Holy Ghost (Romans 14:17). The key to releasing joy is that we cannot allow bad news to get inside of us.

Have you ever been glued to the news media after something horrific happened? I'm reminded of September 11th, 2001, when planes were flown into the Twin Towers in Manhattan, in New York City, which is about five hours from my home in Syracuse, N.Y. Quite honestly, however, on that day it felt like it was right next door! I had to leave the house to do some business and when I came back home my wife met me at the door and said, "We've got problems!" Normally a statement like that only comes up if the plumbing breaks or if we've received a letter from the IRS.

I responded by saying, "What's going on?" My wife responded saying, "The terrorists!"

"Whoa, now listen," I said. "That's the best that they got and you need to stay away from the TV."

Jean Marie instantly realized that she had allowed the news of this world to get inside of her. She lifted up her shield and stopped being glued to the bad news. Remember, the Gospel means the *good* news. Allow me to remind you that the world didn't give you that joy so the world cannot take it away.

Not every negative thing that happens in our lives is from the devil. Sometimes it's just plain old life. I've always said that, "Christians get flat tires too!" However, I do believe that the enemy and his demons are watching and waiting for an opportunity to rip our heart out and rob us of our strength.

The fictional story below is decades old, but still teaches us the value of joy:

SATAN'S GARAGE SALE

One day, the devil had a garage sale. He announced it as a "fire sale" and carefully marked the price upon each item:

Anger: $100
Drunkenness: $400

Drug Addiction: $600
and so on . . .

Each tool sold almost as quickly as it was placed upon the table. But there was one item covered up in the corner with a sign saying, "Not for Sale." Someone remarked, "Nice stuff, but what's that in the corner?"

"I'm sorry," the devil replied, "That tool isn't for sale."

The person became persistent and said, "I want know what that is in the corner!"

The devil narrowed his eyes and hissed, "Sir, I've told you, that tool is not for sale. It is my greatest tool to use on humans."

The man inquired, "Can you at least tell me what it is?"

The devil hissed, picked the tool up in his slimy hand, and put it to the man's chest next to his heart and growled, "It is *discouragement!*"[21]

Man, that sounds pretty creepy, huh?

Discouragement comes from the French word for *dishearten* which means to "cut the heart out."[22] The good news is that the Holy Spirit is called the "Encourager", because He puts the heart back or puts courage back and restores vision. I love the story about the time King David was surrounded with grief after the Amalekites

---

21 According to Google, this story was originally by Don Mondell. I found it on the website http://markwestman.blogspot.com/2010/09/devils-yard-sale.html

22 *Heath's French and English Dictionary*, compiled by James Boïelle, James Bertrand de Vincheles Payen-Payne, published by D. C. Heath, 1903

had taken captive his wives and children and all that he owned, as well as the possessions of his men. That is enough grief to kick the wind out of anyone that I know. Unfortunately, the enemy has no rest to offer, and so it got worse:

> *"And David was greatly distressed; for the people spake of stoning him, because the soul of all the people was grieved, every man for his sons and for his daughters: but David encouraged himself in the Lord his God."*
> **1 Samuel 30:6**

Doesn't it seem that when everything goes wrong, everyone goes after the leader? David did the right thing, because he was a man after God's own heart. He was *discouraged,* but when he went to God, he *encouraged* himself and then the Word of God came to him, giving him a strategy to regain everything.

Are you troubled? Have you taken it to God yet? I personally think that it is very difficult to hear from God when you are troubled. One of the foundation stones for believers is found in Hebrews 6:1, "Faith toward God." This should be in the foundation of every believer. In times of trouble do you call your friends first? No. In times of trouble do you post on Facebook and put all your dirty laundry out there so everyone can be a part of your drama? Definitely no! You have faith toward God. You immediately cry out to your source, your

Heavenly Father.

So don't quit! Have faith toward God and He will give you the strategy you need for the season you are in. You can do it! It's always the darkest just before the dawn. Hang tough. Discipline yourself to keep your eyes on your goal by keeping your eye on the Word, especially if it looks impossible. Jesus said:

> *"…With men it is impossible, but not with God: for with God all things are possible."*
> **Mark 10:27b**

The Psalmist wrote:

> *"…Weeping may last through the night, but joy comes with the morning."*
> **Psalms 30:5b (NLT)**

TWENTY-FOUR HOURS

This is one of the reasons why I generally give myself, and folks under my care, at least twenty-four hours to get their composure after a very complicated day. We have to learn to tap into joy instead of tapping into the world's anxieties, pleasures and distractions. Remember that joy is not a feeling, rather it is a supernatural virtue released by the waters of the well of salvation.

Did you mess up today? Big deal! You're not the only one who did. I exhort you to "cowboy up", and get back in the righteous saddle, so to speak. The longer you stay down, the harder it is to get back up.

If you have sinned, God has a terrific plan for your life. The plan is to help others like yourself who have fallen. Look what David wrote in Psalm 51:12-13:

> *"Restore unto me the joy of thy salvation; and uphold me with thy free spirit. Then will I teach transgressors thy ways; and sinners shall be converted unto thee."*

God wants you to get up so He can use you. "Use me to do what?", you might ask. Look what that last Scripture says, in verse 13, "Then will I teach transgressors thy ways; and sinners shall be converted unto thee."

Now, for your reading pleasure I have listed a few encouraging scriptures pertaining to joy. Please keep your eyes on the Word!

> *"But let all those that put their trust in thee, rejoice: let them ever shout for joy…"*
> **Psalm 5:11a**

> *"Thou wilt show me the path of life. In thy presence is fulness of joy…"*
> **Psalm 16:11a**

> *"And now shall mine head be lifted up above mine enemies round about me: therefore will I offer in his*

tabernacle sacrifices of joy; I will sing, yea, I will sing praises unto the Lord. Hear, O Lord, when I cry with my voice: have mercy also upon me, and answer me."
Psalm 27:6-7

"Let thy priests be clothed with righteousness; and let thy saints shout for joy."
Psalm 132:9

"A merry heart maketh a cheerful countenance: but by sorrow of the heart the spirit is broken."
Proverbs 15:13

"A merry heart doeth good like a medicine: but a broken spirit drieth the bones."
Proverbs 17:22

FOR PERSONAL REFLECTION OR DISCUSSION

- What is difference between being happy and having joy?
- Which one them do you seek the most?
- Is it your spouse's or friend's responsibility to give you joy?
- Have you ever had a circumstance knock the wind out of you? How and when?
- Have you recovered? If so, how?
- Who in your life is responsible for giving you joy?

• Discouragement means, "to take the heart out". What does encouragement mean in this chapter?

LET'S PRAY

Holy Spirit, in Jesus' holy, powerful name, I ask You for a spirit of understanding so I can discern the season that I am in. I ask that I will never lose sight of Your great heart for me. I want to be an encourager, but I know for that to happen I must know how to encourage myself in the Lord. I desire to be used by You, Lord, and to comfort others who are discouraged with the same comfort that You have brought me in times of distress. Thank You for hearing my prayer and for opening my eyes to the fruit of joy in my born-again spirit.
Amen, and so be it.

CHAPTER FIVE

THE BATTLE FOR PEACE

(and how to maintain it when you have it…)

WHEN YOU are tempted, you will always be tempted in one or more of the Spiritual Fronts—that is, areas in which the fruit of the Spirit are growing and working in you. The Spiritual Front of peace is very strategic for Satan, because if he can breakthrough on this front then a door will open that can allow fear, anxiety, depression or a nervous breakdown into your life. So, this chapter is on the fruit of the Spirit of peace, and I am calling it *The Battle for Peace*.

Let's start with a story about a man and his nation. The nation had lost their peace because their enemies would come every year to raid and loot them, causing great poverty in their lives. The Lord sent His angel to visit this man while he was hiding:

> *"When Gideon realized that it was the angel of the LORD, he cried out, "Oh, Sovereign LORD, I'm doomed! I have seen the angel of the LORD face to face!" "It is all right," the LORD replied. "Do not be afraid. You will not die." And Gideon built an altar to the LORD there and named it Yahweh-Shalom (which means, "The LORD is peace")…"*
> **Judges 6:22-24a (NLT)**

Eventually Gideon accepted his role as the leader of Israel after coming to the realization that he was "the man", and by the right hand of God Gideon was instrumental in ushering back in the peace that had been taken from Israel. God revealed to Gideon that He was the God of peace. Gideon and Israel won peace back in what I call a Battle for Peace. They won because they understood the power that peace brings.

You have probably heard it said that nothing is free—and that is quite true. It's the same in the natural and in the spiritual. Peace comes at a price. Someone paid a price for it, someone fought for it. My big question to you is, "Are you willing to fight for your peace?" If you are, then get ready to go into battle for your peace and for the peace of your family!

In the natural we have much freedom in America and

in the free world. God brought this about by having favor on us and on our allies. The price paid was the shed blood of some of our loved ones, but that is expected because freedom is not free.

In the spiritual realm, the battle of the Cross won the battle for peace. Jesus, our Prince of Peace, offered Himself up for our peace. Peace is a product of righteousness— His righteousness. For myself, peace means going to bed knowing that you are right with God. That is because Prince of Peace has infused His peace into our born-again spirit at our new birth.

Let's read what Jesus said:

"I am leaving you with a gift—peace of mind and heart. And the peace I give is a gift the world cannot give. So don't be troubled or afraid."
John 14:27 (NLT)

We must keep fresh the memory of what Christ did for us or we will not appreciate it. Calvary was Ground Zero in the battle for peace. This is one of the reasons why I feel the Lord has prompted me to make the Communion elements available every Sunday for my congregation.

Did you notice that I said "Communion elements" and not, "We will have Communion"? We provide the elements, but it's up to the individual to have true Communion. True Communion is dependent on the attitude and the faith of the individual's heart and their desire to become closer to God. It is not just something that is done to clear the conscience while then going back out into the world with no lingering thought of God and no behavior or character change.

With desire and proper attitude, along with willingness to reform, then and only then can true Communion happen. One denomination calls this the "holy Eucharist". *Eucharist* is a Greek word for "thanks"[23]. We are always to remember what Jesus did on the cross, and to give thanks for the price Jesus paid at Calvary for our peace with God.

Look what the Word has to say regarding this:

"For I have received of the Lord that which also I delivered unto you, that the Lord Jesus the same night in which he was betrayed took bread: And when he had given thanks, he brake it, and said, Take, eat: this is my body, which is broken for you: this do in remembrance of me. After the same manner also he took the cup, when he had supped, saying, This cup is the new testament in my blood: this do ye, as oft as ye drink it, in remembrance of me. For as often as ye eat this bread, and drink this cup, ye do shew the Lord's death till he come."
1 Corinthians 11:23-26

Communion is about reminding ourselves of what

---

23 *eucharístia*, https://www.dictionary.com/browse/eucharist

Jesus did for us. Now, let's look what Jesus accomplished on the cross for us:

> *"But he was wounded for our transgressions, he was bruised for our iniquities: the chastisement of our peace was upon him; and with his stripes we are healed."*
> **Isaiah 53:5**

He was beaten so we can have His peace! Those who know God have a peace and assurance that everything is going to work out. I also want you to know that all the worldly campaigns/songs/displays on "world peace" are not going to do it for us. Yes, nice thoughts and warm songs will sooth our anxiety for a moment, but they don't possess the ability for lasting peace.

There are many organizations that champion peace, and please don't get me wrong, they are great ideas— but they are not all God's ideas of peace. There are also machines and apps that generate relaxing, soothing sounds to help one sense peace, like the sound of waves, falling rain, waterfalls, whale song, and birds chirping in the forest. There are things like spa treatments and aromatherapy that are another temporary way to try to get peace and comfort. Personally, my best aromatherapy is the smell of *Dunkin' Donuts* coffee brewing in the morning! Just messing with you all, but let's look at what Isaiah wrote:

"For unto us a child is born, unto us a son is given: and the government shall be upon his shoulder: and his name shall be called Wonderful, Counselor, The mighty God, The everlasting Father, The Prince of Peace."
Isaiah 9:6

The Hebrew word for *Prince* means, "the head person or the captain that had the rule, chief, general, governor, keeper, lord, ruler, steward."[24] The Hebrew word for *peace—shalom—*means, "to be safe, well, happy, friendly"[25] and also, " good welfare, health, prosperity, and favor." If we put these two words together, the meaning is that Jesus is the captain, ruler or governor making sure that we are being safe, happy, prosperous, full of health, and His favor is on our lives.

Now let's read what the Prince of Peace has to say about peace:

"I am leaving you with a gift—peace of mind and heart. And the peace I give is a gift the world cannot give. So don't be troubled or afraid."
John 14:27 (NLT)

See that? Jesus said, "Don't be troubled or afraid". He is telling us it is within the realm of our authority and responsibility to maintain peace within ourselves.

---

24 Strong's reference: 8269, *sar*

25 Strong's reference: 7965, *shalom*

Believers need to be people of discipline for this peace to remain in us. By "discipline" I mean we need to have a prayer life, a Word life, and should be walking in the Spirit of God's character. Please take time to consider and understand this next statement: If you lose your discipline, you will lose your peace. If you lose faith you will lose your peace.

> *"And the peace of God, which passeth all understanding, shall keep your hearts and minds through Christ Jesus."*
> **Philippians 4:7**

The word *passeth*, in the Greek, means, "to excel and be superior"[26]. It also means "to be a watcher in advance, to mount a guard as a sentinel (post spies at gates); protect: keep with a garrison (troops stationed)."

This definition tells us that if we will yield to the fruit of the Spirit of peace we will be like a guard or sentinel, guarding and protecting our heart (it's a Spiritual Front!) from outside stimuli and then that peace will surpass and excel beyond human expectation.

Is the world going to get any better? My answer to that question is, "Yes and no". Of course, when Jesus comes back we will rule and reign with Him. Until then, Satan knows his time is running short and he is causing as much chaos in the world as he can. Yet God, with His foreknowledge, is using and will continue to use

---

26 Strong's reference: 5242, *huperechó*

what Satan throws at us to His advantage and to bring many to Himself.

The Bible speaks of troubled days ahead:

> *"But as the days of Noah were, so shall also the coming of the Son of man be. For as in the days that were before the flood they were eating and drinking, marrying and giving in marriage, until the day that Noah entered into the ark."*
> **Matthew 24:37-38**

> *"Likewise also as it was in the days of Lot; they did eat, they drank, they bought, they sold, they planted, they builded; But the same day that Lot went out of Sodom it rained fire and brimstone from heaven, and destroyed them all."*
> **Luke 17:28-29**

Child of God, my prayer is that you will understand what I am about to say: Even in the midst of chaos God will preserve His people. He always has and He always will. Receive His peace by faith. Now, let's take a look at this lovely Scripture:

> *"Open the gates to all who are righteous; allow the faithful to enter. You will keep in perfect peace all who trust in you, all whose thoughts are fixed on you! Trust in the* Lord *always, for the* Lord God *is the eternal Rock."*
> **Isaiah 26:2-4 (NLT)**

Jesus is in you so His peace is your peace. It is not your peace—it is Him, or His peace.

"For he is our peace…"
Ephesians 2:14a

Always keep in mind that each fruit of the Spirit reflects the character of Christ and if we do not yield to them and fortify these Spiritual Fronts, we will manifest character flaws. We must either produce peace or we will manifest its counterpart, the works of the flesh. Let's read some antonyms for the word *peace*. These are the counterparts of peace: disharmony, hatred, distress, war, disagreement, agitation. Not good words, are they? I, for one, do not want them to manifest in my life!

There were a number of people in the Bible who lacked the peace of God, but I think King Saul and the disciple Judas top that list in their falls from grace.

The word *peace* comes from the Greek word *eiréné* (pronounced i-ray-nay).[27] This is where we get the English name Irene. In the Greek, *peace* means "prosperity, quietness, rest, and whole".

Godly peace is not a lit scented candle in a room, nor a picnic on a nice day by the lake. It's not one of those mood machines playing the sound of a breeze, or ocean waves cascading on sandy beaches, or birds chirping in the forest. The peace of God is not watching the sun

---

27 Strong's reference: 1515, *eiréné*

set on a warm summer evening, and it is definitely not a visit to a psychic fair. All of those I just listed are counterfeit compared to the peace that God gives His children.

When Jesus told His disciples in John 14:1, "Let not your heart be troubled: ye believe in God, believe also in me," He was instructing them to keep their fleshly, human emotions under the submission of God's Word by faith. He knows that when people lose their peace they get desperate and then they seem to drain the peace from those around them.

But desperation may not be all bad because it can actually create opportunities. For example, the opportunity to stop, think and make a life-changing choice. The choice you make could very well set a flaming course for your destiny, so I suggest that you choose wisely.

During an emotional situation, we can say things that we will regret later. For a comical example, let's look at Burt Reynolds' character Wendell Sonny Lawson in the comedy movie *The End* (hilarious, by the way). Here it is from my memory:

One day Wendell Lawson decided that he was going to end his life once and for all. So, he ran into the ocean and began to swim out as far as his strength would take him. He stopped, and he began to slowly sink under. As he went slowly downward his life began to flash by him a thousand miles a second, and when it came to a standstill he saw his little girl crying, "Daddy, Daddy!"

There was silence as the water surface was beginning to be reflective and still, and suddenly he bursts upward out of the water, gasping for air, all the while yelling out, "I don't want to die, I don't want to die. I want to live, I want to live!" So, Wendell began swimming toward the shore. Obviously, he was exhausted and desperate, and began to think that he wasn't going to make it back alive so he began to negotiate with God.

He said, "Lord, if I make it to shore I will go to church every Sunday. No, I will go to church every day. I will also start giving money to the church, even ten percent of my income; no, fifty percent; No, oh heck, money doesn't mean anything to me so I will give the church all my money."

He continued, "I will also volunteer at the local mission up to twenty hours a week."

As he was swimming he suddenly realized that the shore was reachable and that he was going to make it. He was so happy and was filled with joy, and when he was just a few yards from shore he renegotiated with God. "Hey God, you know, going to church everyday doesn't seem realistic so maybe I will go on Christmas Eve and Easter Sunday. After all, God, you know, who needs a church building—You're everywhere, right?"

"And you know that money thing I talked about? I think ten percent should be enough to give but really, do You seriously need any money? Well, You definitely do not need mine so I'll just keep it for a rainy day." He finished by saying, "Oh yeah, about volunteering all those hours at the mission? Come on, God, you know I don't have the time to do that. I am sure You understand—and You know what, Lord, thank You for saving me. If there is anything you ever need let me know, okay?"

Well, maybe that is a bit much, yet it does sound a little like some of us! My prayer is that, as we protect the spiritual fruit of God's peace, we will never get to the place of wanting to end our lives.

Again, there is a huge difference between experiencing the peace of God and having peace with God. Anyone can sense the peace of God—saint or sinner can come to church and sense His peace. But not everyone can have peace *with* God. That, my friend, would be your first step in understanding peace, because one will never comprehend the power of God's peace without having made their peace with God. Look at this awesome Scripture:

> *"Then justice will dwell in the wilderness, and righteousness (moral and spiritual rectitude in every area and relation) will abide in the fruitful field. And the effect of righteousness will be peace [internal and external], and the result of righteousness will be quietness and confident trust forever. My people shall dwell in a peaceable habitation, in safe dwellings, and in quiet resting-places."*
> **Isaiah 32:16-18 (AMPC)**

Did you notice how long God promises righteousness and peace will last? He said "forever". Righteousness simply means having right standing with God. Peace is a product of righteousness. We have the righteousness of God in our spirit so we can go to bed knowing that we are right with God. Now that is peace that surpasses our understanding!

> *"Therefore, since we have been made right in God's sight by faith, we have peace with God because of what Jesus Christ our Lord has done for us."*
> **Romans 5:1 (NLT)**

This isn't because you prayed some eloquent prayer and it's not because you went to a church, nor because you said three "Our Fathers" and three "Hail Mary's". It's not because you performed some kind of penance (which, by the why, is not found anywhere in the Bible). But rather it's because you have peace with God through what Jesus accomplished on the cross. He died for you—all you did was believe He is the Son of God and accept what He has done for you. That is peace.

Peace comes by having faith in the finished work of the cross of Christ. Because we have peace with God, our conflict with God is over. Although we will still have struggles in the flesh, our biggest struggle will be in maintaining our peace and not allowing condemnation to overtake us and rob us of our peace. We can prevent condemnation by1) acknowledging that you did sin, and 2) receiving His forgiveness immediately.

> *"But if we confess our sins to him, he is faithful and just to forgive us our sins and to cleanse us from all wickedness."*
> ***1 John 1:9 (NLT)***

The word *confess* means, "To agree or concur, to make a confession or to give thanks."[28] Keep this in mind, saint: Do not confess your sin in order to be forgiven, but rather confess or acknowledge your sin because you are thankful that your sin was forgiven— past, present and, yes, future. Now that's good news!

In the same way, parents want their children to acknowledge their wrongs, yet when they do we do not disown them, nor beat them, or cast them away as orphans. Also, as in a marriage or any other relationship, we must acknowledge when we offend each other so that our relationship remains healthy and enriched—that way we don't allow bitterness and resentment to enter our hearts. This will maintain our peace with each other.

In closing this chapter, please understand that we will never be perfect until He comes for us. Until then, we can live our lives in full assurance that we are at peace with the Almighty God, through Jesus Christ His Son, and that we have His peace in our born-again spirit. God

---

28 Strong's reference: 3670, *homologeó*

has empowered us with His character through our new birth, and we must now learn to yield to *His* character and learn to maintain that peace of which He has made us stewards.

FOR PERSONAL REFLECTION OR DISCUSSION

- Have you ever sensed the peace of God?
- Where or when have you felt it?
- What does "peace with God" mean to you?
- Do you feel that you are a person of peace?
- Are you a peacemaker or peacekeeper? What is the difference?

LET'S PRAY

Would you please say this prayer to prepare the way for His Holy Spirit character to be released within you?

Heavenly Father, I declare in the Name of Jesus that I want to strengthen my commitment to You and to bear the fruit of Your Son's character. I do not want to make excuses for my failures, but instead I want to execute righteousness in and through my life for the sake of the Gospel. I know I need you, Holy Spirit. Guide me in this journey and allow me the grace to yield to Your peace, and to usher it in where ever I go. I shod my feet with the preparation of the Gospel of Peace. Thank You for hearing my prayer. Amen.

CHAPTER SIX

THE SUPERNATURAL FORCE OF LONG-SUFFERING

FIRST AND foremost, I would like to say that the subject of long-suffering doesn't mean that we as Christians are destined to live a life of total suffering for a long time! But I would like to make it clear that there may be seasons in our lives when we will have to endure longer than we would like to. My belief is that there is a cost to living for Christ, but the benefits far outweigh the costs. Paul said:

> *"For I reckon that the sufferings of this present time are not worthy to be compared with the glory which shall be revealed in us."*
> **Romans 8:18**

The fruit of long-suffering (also known as patience) is the virtue or Christ-character in us that helps us keep our testimony, our character and our victory. I find this next passage of scripture very satisfying:

> *"For ye were sometimes darkness, but now are ye light in the Lord: walk as children of light: (For the fruit of the Spirit is in all goodness and righteousness and truth;) Proving what is acceptable unto the Lord. And have no fellowship with the unfruitful works of darkness, but rather reprove them."*
> **Ephesians 5:8-11**

Are the fruits of the Spirit of much value to the believer? Again, lets read on:

> *"My fruit is better than gold, yea, than fine gold; and my revenue than choice silver."*
> **Proverbs 8:19**

This reveals the value that the Word of God puts on the fruit of God. If God values spiritual fruit then we should rethink our values. I think there are at least three reasons why Christians do not bear the fruit of the Spirit:

1) Ignorance: No Bible teaching on the subject;

2) Selfishness: They are too into "self", for one reason or another; and

3) Disobedience: They choose to live their life in disobedience to God.

People may choose selfishness unknowingly, or even subconsciously, until they are confronted by a failure, or when some loving person points it out to them (God bless my bride!). The best way to know, I believe, is when we ask the Holy Spirit to get involved with our spiritual growth and He gently reminds or cautions us right before we act out in the flesh.

"This I say then, Walk in the Spirit and ye shall not fulfil the lust of the flesh."
Galatians 5:16

To defend yourself at this Spiritual Front you must choose between:

- The fruit of the Spirit or works of the flesh;
- The character of Christ or character flaws;
- Being the real you or being your alter ego.

We choose to either walk in the Spirit or walk in the flesh. Victory is always a choice. You and I have to choose to yield to the fruit or character that God has placed deep inside our inner man/spirit man at our new birth.

Now this might be a sobering thought to some of you: The life you are living right now consists of all the choices that you have made right up to this very moment. If you do not like the life you are living right now then I suggest you re-evaluate your choices, beginning today.

Of course, there are times when someone else makes a choice that affects your life in a negative way, but the good news is that now you have the privilege to change your life by responding with right choices. After all, it is *your* life. There is a choice that you and I make on a daily basis, whether we will live godly that day or not. Let's get to it!

Where fruit is mentioned in Ephesians 5:9, the Greek word used is *karpos*[29], and the root of this word, in the Greek, is *harpazō*[30], which means "to pluck or to seize" and the root word for *seize* is "to choose for oneself"[31]. So, you see, at the root of bearing fruit is *choice*.

My lovely bride, Jean Marie, is the one who does the grocery shopping (thank God!) and she buys different kinds of fruit to put in our fruit bowl—apples, oranges, plums, pears, bananas, nectarines, whatever's in season,

---

29 Strong's reference: 2590, *karpos*

30 Strong's reference: 726, *harpazó*

31 Strong's reference: 138, *haireó*

of course! My fruit of choice is usually bananas. I find them *"ap-pealing"* (oh yes, I went there!). The point is that I reach out and choose that particular fruit *on purpose*.

It is similar to you and I choosing to yield to the fruit of the Spirit that is needed at the moment. Pay attention now! God empowered your spirit to fulfill what He has called you to do. He also supplied the character you'll need to sustain it. No matter how long and how hard it may seem, by yielding to what He put in you, you will fulfill your assignment here on earth with much joy.

LONG-SUFFERING VS. PATIENCE

The King James version lists the word *long-suffering* as one of the fruits of the Spirit. More commonly it is referred to as *patience*. That interpretation, in and of itself, is not particularly wrong, but it is also not completely accurate.

I've always liked this quote: "If long-suffering had a baby it would be called 'endurance'." That's a great illustration. When a woman conceives a child, it is a long, nine-month journey and then the real pain comes. Her body and emotions suffer a long time, and sometimes the grueling pain of her labor is beyond her ability to bear. So, in a way, the fruit of Spirit of long-suffering can be thought of as operating in a similar manner to how an epidural would help ease suffering in childbirth so the mother can endure all the way to the end.

APPLICATION OF PATIENCE

I think of the need for patience being applied to life as akin to being in a waiting room. As one famous prayer goes: "Lord, give me patience, and give it to me NOW!"

I don't think anyone likes being in a waiting room for a particularly long period of time. It may go something like this (if your temperament is anything like mine): You arrive early and begin to fill out all the necessary paperwork that you did the last time you were there. You find an empty chair and then settle down for what you hope will be a short period of time. You begin by reading the book you brought and eventually get tired of it, so you glance at the clock and say, "Hmmm, not too bad yet."

Next, you turn to a newspaper that happens to be lying there. You quickly put it down after a while because you realize you have no idea whose illness-ridden hands were on it! Then you reach for a magazine, maybe sports or *National Geographic*, or the year's-old women's magazine—because you are now officially getting antsy. The clock is beginning to be your enemy as you reach for your smart phone. You check your email, Fox News, CNN. Then you go check your Facebook app. Then Instagram. Then a quick glance at Twitter because you still have the app even though you don't use it.

By now you realize that the battery on your phone is at 2% and you put it away. You don't even think about reading the Bible because you're starting to get ticked off. Then you perk up when you notice that the person who came in right after you just got called in, and now you're thinking, "What that heck!" You get up and begin pacing the floor like a caged panther, thinking to yourself, "Oh, my God, help me, please don't let me lose it, Lord!" It's the same thing you feel when you get stuck in traffic and you have so much to do or when you're at the DMV. Worse yet, at the checkout line at the supermarket with a trainee working the register. Now this, my friend, is where you apply patience!

But long-suffering is best understood when you're going through a long, painful divorce; or when there is ongoing strife in your home with your spouse or family members; or because of sleeplessness due to a colicky baby or a toddler teething for several nights; or when you have to stay up through most the night waiting for rebellious teenagers to come home so you can make sure they are safe. It's months, or even years, of financial problems due to loss of income, or a forced career change at mid-life with no training in other fields. It's suffering from a long-term sickness or disease, or worse yet when experiencing the sudden death of a loved one. Long-suffering is needed when someone is suffering from a broken heart or dealing with or coming out from an abusive relationship.

This, my friend, is when you and I have to yield every day—several times a day—to long-suffering. You have to protect this Spiritual Front so the enemy cannot take any ground from you. I like to differentiate the two by the illustration below:

LONG-SUFFERING
PATIENCE

You can sum it up by saying that long-suffering is patience stretched. *Long-suffering*, in the Greek, means, "Forbearance or fortitude, patience."[32]. It comes from a root word that means "with long (enduring) temper, patiently". Long-suffering is *patient endurance*. For the rest of us simple folk, let's just sum it up by saying that it is suffering long while continuing to exhibit Christ's character.

We can define *endurance* as "the ability or capacity to do something difficult for a long period of time; the quality of continuing for a long time; the ability to withstand hardship or adversity; especially, the ability to sustain a prolonged stressful effort of activity."[33]

MARATHON

Have you ever run in a marathon? Well I did once, but it's called a 5K where I come from! (Haha, my humor!) Seriously, a marathon is a foot race spanning a course of twenty-six miles, three hundred and eighty-five yards, requiring exceptional endurance. A marriage,

---

32 Strong's reference: 3115, *makrothumia*

33 https://www.merriam-webster.com/dictionary/endurance

parenting, building a business, pastoring a church through difficult times—all of these require exceptional endurance as well.

The writer of Hebrews says:

> *"Wherefore seeing we also are compassed about with so great a cloud of witnesses, let us lay aside every weight, and the sin which doth so easily beset us, and let us run with patience the race that is set before us."*
> **Hebrews 12:1**

The word *patience* is used here but let's look closer. Patience is "cheerful or hopeful endurance"[34]. Did you get that? Cheerful, hopeful endurance. The objective here is not just to endure; it's having endurance with a joyful, hopeful end.

True marathon runners do not stop running at the first sign of rain, or some sniffles, or waking up and just not feeling it that day. No, they are committed from start to finish. They begin with the goal of finishing the race. To them, there is no other option.

Unfortunately, some believers live by their emotions and feelings and not by the Spirit of the Living God. What if the marathon runner just stopped running when they began to feel hot, thirsty or tired? Yet many times we believers sense this self-righteous feeling to quit and we stop running at the first sign of spiritual perspiration.

---

34 Strong's reference: 5281, *hupomoné*

Oh, we quit when it seems too hard, or when we think, "If this were God it wouldn't be so hard." We will reason, "Surely God doesn't expect me to keep this up when it causes me all this effort and perspiration?"

Dear Body of Christ, living victoriously for God is not a fifty-yard dash! Living for God is more like a running in a marathon. Always remember, this is the patience of Jesus living in you. This is the long-suffering of Christ in you that we run on, and here's some really good news: It will never run out as long as you yield to the One who is living in you.

Someone shout, "Put it on!", as the Word says:

"Since God chose you to be the holy people he loves, you must clothe yourselves with tenderhearted mercy, kindness, humility, gentleness, and patience."
Colossians 3:12 (NLT)

"PUT IT ON!"

Believer, stir yourself up when you find yourself in those stressful situations and remember: God is working on your behalf. You are battling on the long-suffering Spiritual Front and you *must* patiently endure, and not be hasty in giving up. Allow me to prophesy over you:

In the Name of Jesus, you will outlast the devil in this situation!

That's because you will continue to yield to the long-suffering of Christ in you, the hope of glory. It will cause you to fight the good fight, as Paul mentioned:

> *"I have fought a good fight, I have finished my course, I have kept the faith."*
> **2 Timothy 4:7**

Before you read this next Scripture, keep in mind that when Paul penned this he, like the other writers of the Word, was under the anointing of the Holy Spirit. Be assured that that he was telling the truth about his experiences in this writing:

> *"Are they Hebrews? So am I. Are they Israelites? So am I. Are they the seed of Abraham? So am I. Are they ministers of Christ? (I speak as a fool) I am more; in labors more abundant, in stripes above measure, in prisons more frequent, in deaths oft. Of the Jews five times received I forty stripes save one. Thrice was I beaten with rods, once was I stoned, thrice I suffered shipwreck, a night and a day I have been in the deep; In journeyings often, in perils of waters, in perils of robbers, in perils by mine own countrymen, in perils by the heathen, in perils in the city, in perils in the wilderness, in perils in the sea, in perils among false brethren; In weariness and painfulness, in watchings often, in hunger and thirst, in fasting often, in cold and nakedness. Beside those things that are without, that which cometh upon me daily, the care of all the churches. Who is weak, and I am*

not weak? Who is offended, and I burn not? If I must needs glory, I will glory of the things which concern mine infirmities. The God and Father of our Lord Jesus Christ, which is blessed for evermore, knoweth that I lie not."
2 Corinthians 11:22-31

Now look what Paul says about his expected reward and ours:

"Henceforth there is laid up for me a crown of righteousness, which the Lord, the righteous judge, shall give me at that day: and not to me only, but unto all them also that love his appearing."
2 Timothy 4:8

Did you read that? "But unto all them also." He's taking about us—we ourselves will receive a crown of righteousness because we endured, we yielded to the fruit of long-suffering (patience).

Have you listened to yourself lately? Are you saying, "I'm so tired, I'm so overwhelmed, I'm just going to give up."?

My loving advice to you is this: Stop it, just stop talking like that! Listen to what the Spirit of God says in His Word:

"So let's not get tired of doing what is good. At just the right time we will reap a harvest of blessing if we don't give up."
Galatians 6:9 (NLT)

There are times like this in life when you have to speak out. Open your mouth and just say, "I can do all things though Christ Jesus who strengthens me. Greater is He that is in me than He that is in the World. No weapon formed against me will prosper. God always causes me to triumph in Christ Jesus. Get out in Jesus Name!" Shout it if you have to!

Yielding to the long-suffering of Christ during very difficult, trying times will help guard your heart and keep your motives pure.

Believer, the Spiritual Front of long-suffering will help prevent unforgiveness from blossoming in your heart. We must humble ourselves and yield to Him.

"Since God chose you to be the holy people he loves, you must clothe yourselves with tenderhearted mercy, kindness, humility, gentleness, and patience. Make allowance for each other's faults, and forgive anyone who offends you. Remember, the Lord forgave you, so you must forgive others. Above all, clothe yourselves with love, which binds us all together in perfect harmony."
Colossians 3:12-14 (NLT)

Long-suffering will help prevent you from the temptation of holding on to insults, envy, bitterness, self-pity, anger and offense against our fellow man, or even God. It is a supernatural force that enables us to walk in the Spirit so we will not fulfill the lust of flesh.

The effects of *not* yielding to long-suffering can be struggles with some deep, emotional, stressful thoughts, or mental anguish that could cause your mind and/or body to suffer the consequences of stress-related symptoms. Your heart will fill with envy, jealousy, resentment or bitterness when our hearts are supposed to be filled with the Holy Spirit.

I personally have met two people who suffered physically and emotionally from not yielding to long-suffering. They lost their joy and their respect for others. They had insomnia, and even their hair had begun to fall out from the anguish. One of them, thankfully, released their unforgiveness and began to enjoy their life again. Unfortunately, the other, as far as I know, has not and continues to suffer, all because they couldn't endure suffering long.

At the end of the Lord's Prayer there's something I'd like to point out, something Jesus said that you may not be aware of:

> *"And forgive us our debts, as we also have forgiven (left, remitted, and let go of the debts, and have given up resentment against) our debtors."*
> ***Matthew 6:12 (AMPC)***

Jesus meant it, and verse thirteen ties into it:

> *"And lead (bring) us not into temptation, but deliver us*

from the evil one…"
Matthew 6:13a (AMPC)

If we do not forgive we will come under the control of the evil one, even if we are saved. The evil one will steal from you, kill and destroy you from the inside out. Verse fifteen sums it up and quite honestly should motivate you to forgive quickly:

"But if you do not forgive others their trespasses [their reckless and willful sins, leaving them, letting them go, and giving up resentment], neither will your Father forgive you your trespasses."
Matthew 6:15 (AMPC)

Wow! You can interpret that any way you want, but I decided to take it at face value.

I would like to pause and share a testimony, and thank God, for He has been so gracious on my behalf. He has given me grace to forgive quickly. My testimony is that I have never, ever hated anyone and I do not hold onto offense for long. Unfortunately, there have been some loving people who have walked out of my life, but I must live by this statement:

"Those who walk out of your life are not connected to your destiny. You love them, and you miss them, but you must live a forward life."

Now this is a great example of long-suffering that is connected to forgiveness. it's found in Matthew

18:21-30 (NLT):

"Then Peter came to him and asked, "Lord, how often should I forgive someone who sins against me? Seven times?" "No, not seven times," Jesus replied, "but seventy times seven! "Therefore, the Kingdom of Heaven can be compared to a king who decided to bring his accounts up to date with servants who had borrowed money from him. In the process, one of his debtors was brought in who owed him millions of dollars. He couldn't pay, so his master ordered that he be sold—along with his wife, his children, and everything he owned—to pay the debt. "But the man fell down before his master and begged him, 'Please, be patient with me, and I will pay it all.' Then his master was filled with pity for him, and he released him and forgave his debt. "But when the man left the king, he went to a fellow servant who owed him a few thousand dollars. He grabbed him by the throat and demanded instant payment." (King James: "Payest thou what you owe me.) "His fellow servant fell down before him and begged for a little more time. 'Be patient with me, and I will pay it,' he pleaded. But his creditor wouldn't wait. He had the man arrested and put in prison until the debt could be paid in full."

So, because the forgiven servant lacked long-suffering, he was not able to overlook his servant's debt.

This is an important principle for us to learn in the

body of Christ, because when we lack the spiritual fruit of long-suffering we do not have the capacity to forgive those who have wronged us. We choose to hang onto debts and offenses for way too long. We live with the expectation of a payday, or an apology from the offender so we can feel vindicated to the whole world. This is all for the sake of us feeling right. You know, I just realized I could put a spin on this. If you do not forgive you will "suffer long"!

I suggest you adopt this perspective—you may never get an apology from someone who wronged you. If you approach them with your offense, don't be offended doubly if they do not see things your way and refuse to give you an apology.

The key is that you did what you were supposed to do—now the rest is on the other party. You are free from that offense, even if they never say they're sorry. Another tip I would like to give you is this: If that person blows up in front of you, step back in your mind and say, "Whatever is going on in them is not coming over onto me."

So, Believer, if you are in this for the long haul in your walk with God, I suggest you learn to walk in the spiritual fruit of long-suffering. Gaining victory at this Spiritual Front will help you form a victorious attitude that the Apostle Paul described in Acts 24:16 (AMPC):

"Therefore I always exercise and discipline myself

[mortifying my body, deadening my carnal affections, bodily appetites, and worldly desires, endeavoring in all respects] to have a clear (unshaken, blameless) conscience, void of offense toward God and toward men."

That is definitely a result of the supernatural force of long-suffering! In Jesus' name, strengthen this Spiritual Front in your life.

FOR PERSONAL REFLECTION OR DISCUSSION

- Do you have a difficult time in a "waiting room"?
- Do you find yourself short tempered when things don't go your way?
- Will long-suffering help you in your relationships— why or why not?
- Is your mind ready for a marathon or a 50-yard dash concerning your walk with God?
- Have you ever hated someone before?
- How do you feel about them now?

LET'S PRAY

Would you please say this prayer to prepare the way for His Holy Spirit and His character to be released within you?

Heavenly Father, I pray in the name of Jesus that

You will help me to strengthen my commitment to you and to bear the fruit of Your Son's character. I have no excuse now, I understand what I must do and I am ready to yield wholeheartedly and passionately to your Spirit. With Your help I will learn to endure through the trials, circumstances and tests that come my way. With Your help I will make it to the end of this marathon called "life". I anticipate hearing, "Well done!" from my Master at the end of my race.

To God be the glory, Amen.

CHAPTER SEVEN

THE GOOD THAT LIES WITHIN

A T CERTAIN times of my life, before I was saved, when my behavior was the worst, my wife Jean Marie would say, "I know that there is some good in him." Even the Syracuse newspaper's special magazine, *The Star Magazine*, quoted her on it! To be completely honest with you, there was *nothing* good in me until Jesus filled my heart with His Spirit and with His character.

Let's begin this chapter with the English translation of the word *goodness* in regards to the fruit of the Spirit.

From Strong's Concordance, the word *goodness* can mean, "Usefulness, morally, excellence (in character or demeanor) gentleness, good(-ness), kindness."[35]

In the same way that our generation has become confused with the word *love*, it has also done the same with the word *good*. Don't be so surprised because the Word of God warned us this would happen:

> *"Woe unto them that call evil good, and good evil; that put darkness for light, and light for darkness; that put bitter for sweet, and sweet for bitter!"*
> **Isaiah 5:20**

What a flip-flop that is! The term "flip-flop" is used in politics when a candidate running for office changes their position on an important issue. We have experienced a great flip-flop in the morality of our country—and world. What God calls evil, there are now legislated laws that say it is good. This is why the goodness of God must be manifested through the light of the Gospel, and not in a judgmental, hypocritical way.

Just like in the natural world where our coastlines are slowing being eroded by the crashing of the ocean waves, so the morality of our nation is slowly being eroding by constant, powerful waves of immorality. But be of good cheer, God has a plan: It's you!

---

35 Strong's reference: 19, *agathosune*

*"For the earnest expectation of the creature waiteth for
the manifestation of the sons of God."*
Romans 8:19

When speaking about the fruit of goodness, we as
believers need to remember that goodness lies within
our born-again spirits. We do not have to groan it out,
grunt it out or squeeze it out. You "yield it out" when
the battle is raging at that Spiritual Front. You don't *know*
God, you *learn* God. Before we can yield to the fruit
of goodness that He put in us, we have to know what
is the goodness of God.

In the first chapter of Genesis, the phrase, "…It was
good," was used six times.

However, in Genesis 1:31, the phrase changes, with
God calling His creation "very good":

*"And God saw every thing that he had made, and,
behold, it was very good. And the evening and the
morning were the sixth day."*

Please know that this was God's definition of "good"
and not a mere man's expression of good. The people
of Israel understood that God was good. Psalms 73:1a
says, "Truly God is good to Israel." So, when someone
came to Jesus and called Him "Good Master", Jesus asked
a question pinpointed at the heart of that person:

"And he said unto him, Why callest thou me good?

*There is none good but one, that is, God: but if thou
wilt enter into life, keep the commandments."*
Matthew 19:17

My question to you now is "Why do *you* call God
good?" Those who know Him have the answer already
in their hearts—it was that goodness that has drawn
us all to Him, as Romans 2:4b says:

*"…not knowing that the goodness of God leadeth thee
to repentance?"*

It was God's goodness that helped us to think differently
about who God is—our misconceptions and perspectives
of what a father is have stunted our thinking. However,
His image as the "good, good Father" comes to light
as we are transformed by the renewing of our mind.

I always use this next passage to help young saints
come to an understanding during those moments when
they are concerned about what is happing in the world.
Many blame God for the bad things in this world.
Questions like: Why do children die of hunger in foreign
lands? Why do people get killed or why did the hurricane
destroy our town? Even insurance companies have a clause
that says "by an act of God", blaming Him for the weather.
Take a look at this:

*"Whatever is good and perfect is a gift coming down to
us from God our Father, who created all the lights in the*

heavens. He never changes or casts a shifting shadow."
James 1:17 (NLT)

Do you need a clearer translation? Allow me to translate: "God = good. Devil = Bad."

The fruit of the Spirit describes characteristics we could never have without the work of the Holy Spirit in our hearts. Goodness is certainly one of them. The Greek word for *goodness—agathosune*—doesn't just refer to an attitude or a motivation, but rather a lifestyle characterized by virtue and helpfulness. To be filled with goodness is to live a life of doing good things for others.

"Even so every good tree bringeth forth good fruit; but a corrupt tree bringeth forth evil fruit."
Matthew 7:17

Granted, there is good in many people. Some only show the good to those they love or those who do them good. Only God can empower us to do good to people we are not connected with in any way, shape or form. When you are in emotional turmoil in your life, when everyone is treating you like dirt, when the kids are crying and the bill collector keeps calling, the spiritual fruit of goodness allows you to stay the course and continue to help others in need. When the battlefront is raging, it is the time to let your light shine.

"A good man out of the good treasure of his heart

bringeth forth that which is good; and an evil man out of the evil treasure of his heart bringeth forth that which is evil: for of the abundance of the heart his mouth speaks."
Luke 6:45

To do a good deed is to treat others justly and also to endorse virtue. The Cub Scouts of America used to have what they called a BobCat pin (now they have a BobCat badge). Back in my day we were instructed to wear our pin upside down each morning and when we do a good deed we can turn it right side up. This would remind each scout to do a good deed every day.

I think, with the Holy Spirit in us, we can turn this up a notch as Jesus shows us in Acts 10:38:

"How God anointed Jesus of Nazareth with the Holy Ghost and with power: who went about doing good, and healing all that were oppressed of the devil; for God was with him."

This means that the Holy Spirit led Jesus and empowered Him to do good. He was anointed to do good. He was anointed to do something and so are we, but the bigger question is: What good have you been anointed to do?

The word for *good* in Acts 10:38 is a Greek word that refers to being a philanthropist[36]. A philanthropist is someone who seeks to promote the welfare of others,

---

36 Strong's reference: 2109, *euergeteó*

especially by the generous donation of money to good causes.

I am so thankful for the goodness of God in the church I have been pastoring for over twenty-seven years. We have rows of people in our church that have given a greater percentage of their earned income than many multimillionaires or billionaires out there.

I thank God for His goodness that has been shown through the hearts of many Christians who support their churches with ten percent of their income, plus the offerings and alms they give on top of that.

Oh, God knows about our generosity *and* the stinginess of our hearts. Let's read about this true story about a poor widow woman:

> *"And there came a certain poor widow, and she threw in two mites, which make a farthing. And he called unto him his disciples, and saith unto them, Verily I say unto you, That this poor widow hath cast more in, than all they which have cast into the treasury: For all they did cast in of their abundance; but she of her want did cast in all that she had, even all her living."*
> **Mark 12:42-43**

God is a rewarder (Hebrews 11:6), not a withholder, as some may think. It is a good thing to be faithful with the blessings God has given us.

"And he said unto him, Well, thou good servant: because thou hast been faithful in a very little, have thou authority over ten cities."
Luke 19:17

When a spirit-filled, fruitful Christian is wronged, they still do good to those who wrong them and do not seek revenge because, well, that is what spirit-filled, fruitful Christians do! We are not filled with revenge but rather, at the Spiritual Front of goodness, we use our greatest weapon and that is love.

"But I say unto you which hear, Love your enemies, do good to them which hate you, bless them that curse you, and pray for them which despitefully use you."
Luke 6:27-28

We cannot be good on our own. God alone defines goodness and, as Jesus said, "No one is good except God alone." (Mark 10:18b, ESV) The goodness that God gives cannot come from human effort alone. Even Paul, a Pharisee of the strictest order, could not force every part of his person to embody goodness. He writes in Romans 7:18-19:

"For I know that in me (that is, in my flesh,) dwelleth no good thing: for to will is present with me; but how to perform that which is good I find not. For the good that I would I do not: but the evil which I would not, that I do."

As the Spirit produces the fruit of goodness in us, we become "salt and light". Then, goodness will overcome evil. Our expressions of goodness can help diminish the effects of evil in the world.

As the writer of Romans says,

"And I myself also am persuaded of you, my brethren, that ye also are full of goodness, filled with all knowledge, able also to admonish one another."
Romans 15:14

God's goodness will grow in us as we yield and will not stop until we see Jesus—and then we will be like Him.

"Being confident of this very thing, that he which hath begun a good work in you will perform it until the day of Jesus Christ."
Philippians 1:6

God breathed into and inspired the Scriptures so that we can be completely equipped "for every good work." As you read the Word, you may be inspired to take necessary steps to move forward in the area that God has been prompting you about. As you are reading, studying and applying the Word, His goodness will inspire you to go on. After all, isn't that what inspire means? In Spirit!

God is good. Through the work of the Holy Spirit in us, God reproduces His goodness in our hearts, and it is manifested through our lives. His goodness enables us to live our lives characterized by the desire to do good for the everyday benefit of others. Saint and sinner alike will see the work of God in us and God will receive all the glory.

There is nothing wrong with taking credit for something. People do it all the time. Some think it is pride. I do not agree as long as the attitude is Christ-like. At the end of a movie you will see all of these names credited for their part in the making of that movie. God doesn't mind us taking credit, but do not touch His glory. Your Father in heaven rejoices in your good works.

"Let your light so shine before men, that they may see your good works, and glorify your Father which is in heaven."
Matthew 5:16

WOULD THE APOSTLE PETER RAISE YOU FROM THE DEAD?

In the book of Acts there is a story about a woman who died, a good woman who did good deeds. Her name was Tabitha. Let's read:

"Now there was at Joppa a certain disciple named Tabitha, which by interpretation is called Dorcas: this woman was

full of good works and almsdeeds which she did. And it came to pass in those days, that she was sick, and died: whom when they had washed, they laid her in an upper chamber. And forasmuch as Lydda was nigh to Joppa, and the disciples had heard that Peter was there, they sent unto him two men, desiring him that he would not delay to come to them. Then Peter arose and went with them. When he was come, they brought him into the upper chamber: and all the widows stood by him weeping, and shewing the coats and garments which Dorcas made, while she was with them. But Peter put them all forth, and kneeled down, and prayed; and turning him to the body said, Tabitha, arise. And she opened her eyes: and when she saw Peter, she sat up. And he gave her his hand, and lifted her up, and when he had called the saints and widows, presented her alive. And it was known throughout all Joppa; and many believed in the Lord. And it came to pass, that he tarried many days in Joppa with one Simon a tanner."
Acts 9:36-43

Now Luke, the writer of Acts, painted a picture of a very noble, generous woman whom the community loved and would have dearly missed at her passing—thus the weeping. She had a talent with the spinning wheel and with it she made lovely garments and coats for many. (Coats were undergarments worn tightly to the skin. Garments were worn over the coats.)

It reminds me of the time we gave clothing away at

our Outreach Center. A young teenaged girl tried on a dress and she felt so happy and pretty that she twirled in her new dress and said, "I have an Easter dress now!" Seeing that sort of response moves my heart. Solid Rock Outreach was a Dorcas/Tabitha that day. The story in Acts doesn't mention that Dorcus said one word, yet everyone around her wept and sang her praise for the life she had lived.

Shouldn't that be the way we live also? We need to do better at allowing others to pat us on the back and say "thank you" instead of us doing it ourselves.

The writer of Proverbs wrote:

"Let someone else praise you, not your own mouth—a stranger, not your own lips."
Proverbs 27:2 (NLT)

Luke also gave Dorcas one of the highest honors that one would have—He called her a "disciple". That's right, a *disciple*. To be a disciple is a great responsibility. Switching the components of the word "responsibility" around helps bring it to full meaning: *the ability to respond.* Dorcas served with passion before she died and I can only imagine that her passion and enthusiasm for serving people and sharing the goodness of God went to a whole new level after she was raised from the dead. What about you? What have you done to serve the Lord that is so important, so *necessary* that He would raise you from the dead to continue the work? That's a question we should all ask of ourselves daily!

> *"So let's not get tired of doing what is good. At just the right time we will reap a harvest of blessing if we don't give up. Therefore, whenever we have the opportunity, we should do good to everyone—especially to those in the family of faith."*
> **Galatians 6:9-10 (NLT)**

FOR PERSONAL REFLECTION OR DISCUSSION

- Based on how you touch others, would there be any reason to raise you up from the dead like Peter did for Dorcas?

- If yes, make a list of reasons and share it with someone—or better yet, ask someone else to write the list.

- Did you ever seek revenge on someone? Have you stopped?

- What is the meaning of the word "goodness" in this chapter?

- Fill in the blank: "Well done, thou _____ and faithful servant."

DECLARATION

I declare that the only goodness in me is the goodness that God put in me!

LET'S PRAY

Father God, I would like to thank You for being a good, good Father to me. Also, thank You for saving me and empowering me with Your character. I am sorry for neglecting to yield to what You put in me. Now I ask You, in Jesus' Name, that by the leading of the Holy Spirit You will help me to bear the fruit of the Holy Spirit. I ask this so I can strengthen the nine Spiritual Fronts in my life and continue to see You do good through me. Lord, I also ask You to allow me to flow in Your goodness every day and at every opportunity.
Amen.

CHAPTER EIGHT

THE GENTLE GIANT

IN THIS chapter I would like to impart some wisdom regarding the "Gentle Giant" that lives in you. Again, let's look at the ingredients that God put in us:

> "But the fruit of the Spirit is love, joy, peace, longsuffering, gentleness, goodness, faith, meekness, temperance: against such there is no law."
> **Galatians 5:22-23**

Gentleness, in the Greek, means, "Usefulness, morally, excellence in character or demeanor, gentle or kind."[37]

---

37 Strong's reference: 5544, *chréstotés*

In most circles, being tough and looking tough is a way of life. I think it takes a really strong person to be truly gentle. Henry Wadsworth Longfellow gives us a wonderful illustration of gentleness in his poem *The Village Blacksmith*. The main character is described this way:

> *The smith, a mighty man is he,*
> *With large and sinewy hands;*
> *And the muscles of his brawny arms*
> *Are strong as iron bands.*[38]

However, the poem goes on and, in church, he hears his daughter singing a hymn, and the blacksmith is overcome with emotion:

> *And with his hard, rough hand he wipes a tear out of his eyes.*

This is an example of gentleness. This is might restrained, humility and grace applied.

I found the phrase "gentle giant" in the Merriam-Webster dictionary and it paints a picture of someone who is tall and strong, but also has a quiet mild nature about themselves. Someone who is thoughtful and caring for others[39]. Don't you think that this describes our

---

38 The full version of Longfellow's poem can be found at http://www.hwlongfellow.org/poems_poem.php?pid=38

39 https://www.merriam-webster.com/dictionary/gentle%20giant

friend Jesus? When Jesus was on the earth He was someone who could have wiped out humankind with one word out of His mouth. As He was jeered while suffering and bleeding to death on the cross, He could have made it stop. The crowd jeered, "If you are the Son of God then come down off that cross and we will believe You." It's easy for us now to look back and see how foolish the crowd was.

There is a natural gentleness and there is supernatural gentleness

I am speaking about the supernatural goodness of Jesus. He was, and is still, the gentlest, kindest person that has ever walked the face of this earth. This is the same kind, gentle spirit that He put in our born-again spirit, one that we must show others even when we do not want too!

After killing six people and wounding seven in a year-long rampage in New York City, one of the biggest manhunts in the history of America ended on August 15th, 1977. Murderer David Berkowitz was apprehended. In a prison interview with CBN, Berkowitz said, "Well, the past, the scars of the past are always going to remain and haunt me. But I've given my life to Jesus Christ. And He has let me know in His Word that He has forgiven me completely. All my sins are washed away."[40]

Since David gave his life to Jesus Christ he has refused to be paroled and refused to be call the "Son of Sam", but

---

40 Full interview found at http://www1.cbn.com/700club/son-sam-becomes-son-hope

instead "Son of Hope". He went from prison troublemaker to model inmate. Berkowitz now serves others in prison and ministers in chapel services. 'A Pace Law Review 2011 entry by Rebekah Binger published recently, titled *Prison Ain't Hell: An Interview with David Berkowitz*, uses Berkowitz's in-prison salvation story to make a case for state-funded, faith-based prison rehabilitation programs, that they do not violate the Establishment Clause. She boldly states, "This story must not be dismissed or ignored."' [41]

I share this story to illustrate that when God gets a hold of someone He does a really good job in them! The hardest criminal heart can become soft and gentle when they receive Christ and begin to yield to His character. I'd like to remind you of this: God doesn't empower your character; rather He empowers you with *His* character. We need to yield to His character and not to the works of the flesh or to those of our past. Yes, even when it is contrary to the very core of our flesh, we must yield to the kindness and gentleness of Christ.

Gentleness is a requirement when we confront sin in other people's lives. Paul wrote:

"Dear brothers and sisters, if another believer is overcome by some sin, you who are godly should gently and humbly

---

[41] Quote found at https://www.christianpost.com/news/son-of-sam-serial-killer-wont-seek-parole-gives-jesus-as-reason-54474/

help that person back onto the right path…"
Galatians 6:1a (NLT)

Please note that Paul begins with, "Dear brothers and sisters . . ." He is instructing *us*, the Church. Doesn't it seem sometimes that we show more kindness and gentleness to those outside of our own church family?

Paul goes on to say, "If another believer is overcome by sin, you who are godly [spiritual] should gently and humbly help that person back onto the right path." I think that sometimes we forget where we come from. Listen, friends, you and your family are not perfect, same as me, because, like us, we all have flesh.

The King James version of Galatians 6:1 says, "You who are spiritual restore such a one." You cannot restore someone when you are emotionally wrapped up in the person's failure. You may have to step back and process your emotions and yield to fruit of the Spirit of kindness and gentleness.

It is important that we yield to God's spiritual fruit when confronting people who have sinned and not do take any action from our flesh. Otherwise we could cause lasting harm to someone's faith. Saying things like, "You have sinned against God, how could you do such a thing like that?" or "What in the world is the matter with you? You blew it, my friend, and it's over for you. You're done, finished and you will never be trusted again," are not going to help toward any kind of restoration.

Consider conducting the restoration process this way, with the gentleness and kindness of our Lord Jesus: "How are you doing? How's your family handling this? I want you to know we're here for you. Please know that God loves you just as much now as He did before you stumbled and fell. He died for that and has already forgiven you, so please do not allow the devil or anyone else to condemn you . . . but let's begin by claiming the promises of restoration in your life."

"Let your gentleness be evident to all. The Lord is near."
Philippians 4:5 (NIV)

Gentleness and kindness will always be revealed in how you present yourself to people, how you handle yourself and how you speak to them, and even how you listen to their side of the story. James says:"

"Wherefore, my beloved brethren, let every man be swift to hear (give audience), slow to speak, slow to wrath (violent passion): For the wrath (violent passion) of man worketh not the righteousness (character) of God."
James 1:19-20 (clarifications mine)

I sense that the time we spend in God's presence and in His Word will determine how quickly we yield to the fruit of the Spirit—the more time, the quicker we yield.

"People is ministry and ministry is people"—it may not be proper English, but this is one of the leadership

lessons in my church's Faith Family Institute, called Discipleship 1. We say that if you feel the call to lead, but you do not like people, then go and buy some dogs and lead them instead!

Yielding to the character of Christ through the fruit of the Spirit begins at home. I know it can be very difficult sometimes at home, but God knows best and He set you in that family for a purpose—and that purpose is to be salt and light. We're also set into families to be taught and to learn the ways of the Lord by godly parents or the people you live with. "Who is my family?", you may ask. Your family are the people who are in your life.

Of course, it's not easy. When dealing with the people in our lives—whether at work, play or church—we must learn how to gently handle different situations in trying times. I share this analogy often when providing training for my ushers and leaders, drawn from John Maxwell's book *Winning With People*. If there is a fire (but here I am speaking about the people or situations in your life) you can approach that fire with a bucket in each hand—one bucket is filled with gasoline and the other bucket is filled with water. Now whatever bucket you use on that fire will determine what you are left with.[42]

Be determined to be kind and gentle with all of the people you come across everyday: The store clerk, the

---

42 John C. Maxwell, *Winning With People: Discover the People Principles that Work for You Every Time*, (Nashville, TN: Thomas Nelson, Inc., 2004), p147.

waitress at the diner or Starbucks. Be especially determined with your children when they come home from school.

Many years ago, when my youngest daughter Danielle was about five-years-old, we were at the dinner table and her older sister Shannon told us that Danielle was telling all of our neighbors that her mom and dad drank beer and smoked all the time. I know she was doing this because she wanted to fit in. I looked at Danielle in shock and said, "Danielle, why would you say something like that?" She responded with tears in her eyes, "Well, you don't know what's inside of me!"

I just heard recently that her own five-year-old daughter, Ava, said the same thing to her! The moral of the story is that you and I do not know what people, children, or even your family, are going through. Have you ever seen someone break down and cry after a simple little thing? Obviously, there is more going on with them than what you thought, something that goes much deeper than the outburst. We do not know where people have come from, or what they have been through. So, make a decision, now, that you are going to treat everyone with some Aretha Franklin R E S P E C T.

Jesus was gentle to people this way also. Matthew wrote:

"A bruised reed shall he not break..."
Matthew 12:20a

You cannot know a person more than Jesus knows

them, unless of course God gives you discernment or a word of knowledge. However, for the religious folk, Jesus would keep hitting them right between the eyes! Practice being a gentleman, a gentlewoman. Be kind to people even when they are not kind to you. Remember the Golden Rule? That was taken right out of the Bible:

"Do to others whatever you would like them to do to you. This is the essence of all that is taught in the law and the prophets."
Matthew 7:12 (NLT)

You will be surprised at how much your children learn from you just by watching you in public. I'd like to share a story with you that I once heard about a taxi driver:

A young couple was leaving the airport in a foreign country and they waved down a taxi to take them to their hotel. The traffic was horrendous—cars were beeping and dodging in and out, putting other cars and pedestrians in constant danger. Suddenly, a car deliberately and maliciously pulled out in front of the taxi and the driver had to slam on his brakes or he would have smashed into it. The luggage, papers, cell phones, all went flying forward. Then, the person who pulled in front of them rolled down his window and began to cuss and swear. The taxi driver calmly and gently just waved his hand back to him.

The wife said to the cab driver, "How can you be so

calm and gentle with him after what he did?" The taxi driver simply said, "My dad taught me that there are many people who are like garbage trucks and they will try to dump their garbage on you. My dad told me, 'Just refuse to receive their garbage, and enjoy your day."

Now that is good, but let's learn from the best now. One of the greatest learning tools you and I have is the yoke of Christ. This is why I say, "You do not know God, but rather you 'learn' God." God is big and powerful, and yet soft and gentle. We see His yoke as Matthew writes of it in 11:29-30 (NIV):

> *"Take my yoke upon you and learn from me, for I am gentle and humble in heart, and you will find rest for your souls. For my yoke is easy and my burden is light."*

The writer of Romans gives us an insight into how we can tap into the yoke of Christ and keep from doing the wrong thing. He says:

> *"Neither yield ye your members as instruments of unrighteousness unto sin: but yield yourselves unto God, as those that are alive from the dead, and your members as instruments of righteousness unto God. For sin shall not have dominion over you: for ye are not under the law, but under grace."*
> **Romans 6:13-14**

Synonyms for the word *yield* are: "To submit, let go, surrender to, give way, fold and come to terms with."

Keep in mind that we are speaking about a powerful God who has the ability to be very soft and kind to us. We're accustomed to thinking of power and strength as being opposite to gentleness, softness and tenderness. Yet this is not always true.

Did you know that during the First World War, British fighter pilots came up with an amazing idea, based on a discovery in the previous century[43] that thick layers of silk stopped low velocity shrapnel better than a metal plate? They wrapped silk around their heads and then wore leather horse riding helmets on top of the silk, giving them extra protection should their plane come under fire whilst in flight.

Scientists still aren't sure just what it is that gives silk its strength, but it's true—in certain situations soft, gentle, tender silk can prove far stronger than cold, hard metal.

Jesus showed us that the same holds true for human character. Some people try to make themselves impenetrable to the people around them. Jesus showed us that gentleness, a heart that is soft toward others, and tenderness, are in fact qualities of great strength!

So, when you get that urge to show how powerful and

---

strong you are, remember to yield to the spiritual fruit of gentleness and let that Gentle Giant come out of you.

FOR PERSONAL REFLECTION OR DISCUSSION

- Are there people you know who are strong but kind? Name two of them.

- Have you changed since the day you received Christ? How?

- Give at least one example of when you yielded to kindness/gentleness instead of showing your strength.

- Can you share an example in the Bible of when Jesus showed kindness?

- Fill in the blank: God did not empower our character, but rather He empowered us _____ _____ _____.

DECLARATION

I declare in the Name of Jesus that I will yield to the fruit of kindness/gentleness to everyone I meet, but especially with my family.

LET'S PRAY

Father God, thank You so much for loving me and for being so kind to me. You loved me before I loved You. You could have wiped me off the face of this planet, but You showed so much kindness, and have been so gentle to me, and for that I am so grateful. Jesus,

my gratefulness will not be demonstrated by mere lip service, but by my actions—with the help of the Holy Spirit, of course.
Amen.

CHAPTER NINE

THE ASSASSINS OF FAITHFULNESS

IN THIS chapter[44], I would like to take a different approach with teaching on the fruit of Spirit of faithfulness. This Spiritual Front is a battle line that the enemy desires to win at all costs. He wants to destroy how you are perceived by those around you. He knows if he can get you to compromise your witness, take the

---

44 Much of the content of this chapter was inspired by teaching I heard many years ago, as a young Christian. I can't remember the speaker who originally taught on the Assassins of Faithfulness, it's been so long, but these principles have become an intrisic part of my own walk of faith and ministry, and I share them here partly to honor the saint of God that unknowingly inspired and instructed me.

saltiness out of your words, cause your light to dim in the eyes of those who are lost, your effectiveness will be diminished.

He will use multiple schemes to do so and if we are not strong in the Lord and in the power of His might, our character may be subject to an assassination. This could cause setbacks in your life, along with lost opportunities and broken relationships.

I have found the best, and maybe the most proper way, of receiving promotion from the Lord is to remain faithful to Him and to others in your life. If you are looking for a spiritual promotion, please do it the right way! Keep in mind that promotion in the world works differently than it does in the kingdom of God. There is the right way to be promoted and the wrong way— it all comes down to motive. Matthew writes:

> *"Then James and John, the sons of Zebedee, came over and spoke to him. 'Teacher,' they said, 'We want you to do us a favor.' 'What is your request?' he asked. They replied, 'When you sit on your glorious throne, we want to sit in places of honor next to you, one on your right and the other on your left.' But Jesus said to them, 'You don't know what you are asking! Are you able to drink from the bitter cup of suffering I am about to drink? Are you able to be baptized with the baptism of suffering I must be baptized with?' 'Oh yes,' they replied, 'We are able!' Then Jesus told them, 'You will*

indeed drink from my bitter cup and be baptized with my baptism of suffering. But I have no right to say who will sit on my right or my left. God has prepared those places for the ones he has chosen.'"
Mark 10:35-40 (NLT)

James and John wanted to secure their legacy with a position of honor before men. (Well, to be fair to them, it was actually their mother pushing for a promotion. See Matthew 20:21) They wanted to secure a legacy in the new kingdom. An interesting note is that, according to Jesus, they were more than willing to share in the necessary persecutions to do so—especially, and I emphasize *especially*, if it would secure them this particular place of honor.

Jesus, knowing them and knowing their future, acknowledged that they were correct in saying that they would join Him in His suffering. Unfortunately for James and John, He could not and would not promise them the promotion they wanted. That is because it had already been established before the foundation of the world by His Father.

The question isn't whether or not we will be rewarded for our faithfulness, for the Scripture is clear that God rewards those who have been counted faithful. The real question is, what is the motive behind our serving? If your motive is pure then your faithfulness will bear its fruit and promotion will follow.

WHAT IS YOUR MOTIVATION?

What is your motive for serving in your church? To help you, here is a question to ask yourself: "Am I willing to endure hardship, even though it may not result in the position or promotion that I desire?" Did you know that many young men and women who have enlisted in the U.S. Armed Forces are told, at recruitment, that they will be able to go into a certain specialized field? Unfortunately, after boot camp, most don't get the position that they desired. That happens more often than one would think when young recruits are eagerly signing up in the recruiting office. Yet that doesn't change their commitment to serving in the Armed Forces because they took an oath to serve their country no matter what.

What was the motive behind the selfless serving of the Apostle Paul, concerning his commitment to the Gospel?

> *"I do all this for the sake of the gospel, that I may share in its blessings."*
> **1 Corinthians 9:23 (NIV)**

YOU NEED ENDURANCE

What a man, what an apostle! Paul was a man who taught what he lived and lived what he taught. He shares his character-building, spirit-filled philosophy with his son in the faith, Timothy:

> *"Endure suffering along with me, as a good soldier of*
> *Christ Jesus. Soldiers don't get tied up in the affairs of*
> *civilian life, for then they cannot please the officer who*
> *enlisted them."*
> **2 Timothy 2:3-4 (NLT)**

There are two things this passage tells us that a soldier of Jesus needs to learn: First, we need to learn how to endure, and second, we need to learn how to avoid distractions.

The Strong's Concordance says that *to endure* means, "To undergo hardship, to be afflicted, to endure afflictions and to suffer trouble."[45]

This is a facet of faith that Abraham had called "enduring faith". Abraham's life was the life of an Old Testament soldier journeying through the land and receiving the blessed life. He was consistent and faithful in his walk with God.

Some will say that "practice makes perfect", but the reality is that if you are practicing something incorrectly it will come out incorrectly. That includes our personal lifestyle. If we are practicing our faith incorrectly the results will be revealed. I say many times, "Some people practice law and some practice medicine, so for crying out loud, we have a right to 'practice Christianity'!" Even

---

45 Strong's reference: 2553, *kakopatheó*

if we practice it correctly we can get some things wrong and that's understandable, because no one is perfect. The reward of living a consistent, faithful Christian life allows us to leave a legacy for our children and grandchildren. I encourage you to walk worthy of your calling.

Let me share the story of a teen who unfortunately experienced the consequences of doing things the wrong way. There was a lady who attended my former church and one day she came over to our house to fellowship. She told me a story that I will never forget concerning her parents who were Christians:

On Sundays they sang in the choir, ushered and even served as deacons. Every Sunday they went to church to sing, worship and shout praise to God. But when they got home they yelled and screamed at each other, cussed, smoked and got drunk. Then on Sunday morning they got in the car and went back to church to praise the Lord.

Needless to say, her parents' marriage began to fall apart and she was eventually sent to a foster home. The old woman went on to tell me that she ended up in another Christian home. On Sundays her foster family also went to church, sang in the choir, ushered, and even served as deacons. They didn't miss a Sunday to sing, worship and shout praises to God. But when they got back home they *continued* to sing, speak wholesome words and pray.

She told me that her observation of her foster family blew her mind. She thought her own parents had been living the Christian life until she experienced life with people who were truly living a consistent, faithful Christian life.

I don't know about you, but that made me very sad. I am sure that there are countless other families living in a similar way out there also. Allow me to exhort you with what Paul said:

> *"I therefore, the prisoner for the Lord, appeal to and beg you to walk (lead a life) worthy of the [divine] calling to which you have been called [with behavior that is a credit to the summons to God's service, living as becomes you] with complete lowliness of mind (humility) and meekness (unselfishness, gentleness, mildness), with patience, bearing with one another and making allowances because you love one another."*
> **Ephesians 4:1-2 (AMPC)**

Listen: Having consistent positive Christian habits in your life will help you to live a productive life.

Faithfulness will create opportunities and help you achieve unbelievable goals in all areas of life including physical fitness by faithful exercise, receiving diplomas by being faithful to your assignments, and getting raises and promotions because of your spirit of excellence.

DON'T GET DISTRACTED

Also, because you have been faithful to your commitment to prayer, you will see answered prayers in your life.

When a soldier does not endure he will be given to distraction. *Distraction* means "mental distress or derangement, division or disorder."[46] Distracted people are prone to worry and anxiety. Whenever I think of being caught up into distraction, good ol' Martha comes to mind.

Luke writes about Martha and Mary, the sisters who hosted Jesus for dinner in their home. Please note that Jesus, the Son of God, was in the house! He wasn't just in the house, He was teaching in the house, imparting His spiritual influence in the living room. That to me is like saying, "Drop everything, my favorite TV show, *Jesus is Alive*, is on!"

However, Martha got distracted from what was most important. Hopefully she got the message Jesus shared with her. Let's read:

> *"And Jesus answered and said unto her, Martha, Martha, thou art careful and troubled about many things: But one thing is needful: and Mary hath chosen that good part, which shall not be taken away from her."*
> **Luke 10:41-42**

Mary recognized the importance of the moments that Jesus was in her home and she sat at His feet so she would hear something concerning her future. Do not get distracted with everything else going on in your life, but stay focused on Who is really important. You may ask,

---

46 https://www.dictionary.com/browse/distraction

"How can I do this?"

"We do this by keeping our eyes on Jesus, the champion who initiates and perfects our faith…"
Hebrews 12:2a (NLT)

Now let's discuss the "Assassins of Faithfulness". I am not putting them in any particular order because every person is wired differently. For sure there are many more, but here I will cover six of the most significant. I have already mentioned three of them in this chapter—Wrong Motive, Lack of Endurance, and Distraction (although I'm going to expand on that one shortly). Here are three more: Quitting, Procrastination and Discontentment.

QUITTING

Quitting simply ends everything. Similar to suicide or abortion, quitting produces no hope and no new life. As the saying goes, "Quitters never win." It is truly sad in every way. Never give up!

I want you to know that there is an ingredient that can work towards the betterment of your success. It is widely unwanted, but it may be the necessary evil that will lead you to the better you and to a better life. The dictionary tells us that *failure* is, "An action or thing that proves unsuccessful."[47] Drop the mic on that one and walk away!

---

47 https://www.dictionary.com/browse/failure

Allow me to clarify—I am not insinuating that you go out today and fail. God forbid! What I am saying is, when failure does come, look at it through the eyes of God to get the bigger picture. Failure can bring devastation upon a person's life. That isn't necessarily bad. In my opinion, there is only thing that can lead someone out of failure or devastation and that is a vision or hope for the future. The Word says, "Where there is no vision, the people perish." (Proverbs 29:18a)

God's perspective of our failure and devastation is so much different from ours. My advice for you is to step back into His presence and get *His* perspective of your life. When there are problems or failures, what we can't do is ignore them or try and paper over them. Sometimes it is better to step away of a situation for a time, get a new perspective—a faith perspective, based on the promises of God—and then, when we are ready, step back into situation with the solution to the problem.

Perspectives shift in the presence of God. The eyes of faith will allow you to look at your problems the way God looks at them and impart faith into the process. God can use your failure to motivate you, to raise your game, to help you take inventory of your life's attitude and even create an opportunity to redirect the course of your life. By asking God for help you can increase the capacity in your spirit, soul and body.

There are great people all around the world, in every walk of life who have failed. Did you notice that

I didn't call them "losers"? Only one thing will qualify you to labeled as a loser: quitting.

Michael Jordan didn't make the team the first time.

Abraham Lincoln suffered decades of loss and failure before becoming one of the most influential presidents in U.S. history.

Jim Carry is a successful actor but we don't all know the story of Carrey's struggle. He grew up in a low-income family with a father who struggled to keep jobs. They were so poor that he had to drop out of high school at the age of fifteen and get a job as a janitor, just to help support the family. At his first stand-up routine, at a club called Yuk Yuk's in Toronto, he was booed off stage. Later, when he auditioned for Saturday Night Live for the 1980-81 season, he failed to land any part. Yet we all know the rest of the story—up to now, that is.

Dr. Ben Carson, a renowned neurosurgeon who once ran for president, grew up in a single-parent home, abandoned by his bigamist father, in a poor, inner city ghetto, was greatly mocked at school for his inability to thrive academically went on to overcome his struggles and become a foremost doctor, author and politician.

Bill Gates was Harvard's most successful drop out, but that didn't stop him from being faithful to his dreams.

"Success it not final, failure is not fatal, it is the courage to continue that counts."
Winston Churchill

Always humorously remember, too, that even at your conception you were a winner. Science teaches that there are over 250 million sperm cells released during sex from the male. Now think about that—you out-swam 249,999 other sperm cells! Your little tail just fluttered and fluttered and then bang! You crossed the finish line turning around to your potential siblings and said, "In your face!" Ok, maybe that last part didn't happen, but you won.

Concerning our failures, please know that God is always working behind the scenes for your benefit. The writer of Romans says:

> *"And we know that God causes everything to work together for the good of those who love God and are called according to his purpose for them. For God knew his people in advance, and he chose them to become like his Son, so that his Son would be the firstborn among many brothers and sisters."*
> **Romans 8:28-29 (NLT)**

PROCRASTINATION

Procrastination is described in the dictionary as "An act or habit of putting off or delaying something requiring immediate attention."[48] I have felt in my heart to teach and write on the subject of procrastination for a very long

---

48 https://www.dictionary.com/browse/procrastination

time. I was supposed to teach on it for the last several years and most definitely, just maybe I will get it done by next year! (I hope you realize what I just wrote was just a humorous illustration of what procrastination is.)

Listen to this: In some areas of our lives procrastination can develop into a major character flaw. For example, if you repeatedly say that you are going to do something for somebody by a certain date or time and you do not meet the deadline, the other person has the right to say that you lied.

Someone once came to me and called another person a liar. I was shocked to hear that accusation and told them that the person they had accused had never lied to me in all the years I'd known them. In fact, I was having trouble with their harsh, judgmental statement. Then, the accuser told me about several things that this person had said he would do, yet continually pushed the dates back for getting them done. Soon after this conversation, others came forward and told me of similar, disturbing details. Do you see how procrastination can become a character flaw in one's life? If you are repeatedly missing deadline after deadline, you may be compromising your integrity to other people and this, my friend, if not dealt with can eventually assassinate your character.

DISTRACTIONS

As we've discussed, a distraction is anything that prevents a person from giving their full attention to something or someone, and can lead to extreme agitation of the mind or emotions:

> *"But Martha was cumbered about much serving, and came to him, and said, Lord, dost thou not care that my sister hath left me to serve alone? Bid her therefore that she help me. And Jesus answered and said unto her, Martha, Martha, thou art careful and troubled about many things: But one thing is needful: and Mary hath chosen that good part, which shall not be taken away from her."*
> **Luke 10:40-42**

Distractions will try to engage your full attention. What we need is "blinders" to keep our focus straight ahead. Horse blinders reduce vision for the horse wearing them, from 180° to as little as 30°. Blinders help horse can focus on its task, whatever that may be. If a believer's mind is not properly harnessed, distractions will then create an even larger problem: discontentment. This can be bad news for those who want to please God and walk worthy of their calling.

DISCONTENTMENT

Discontentment means, "To have a lack of contentment, dissatisfied, a restless desire or craving for something one does not have."[49] Distractions will try to engage your

---

49 https://www.dictionary.com/browse/discontentment

full mental attention so they can have an opportunity to create discontentment in your heart. Discontentment springs up from the dissatisfaction you may have with the circumstances of your life. Discontentment is the belief that God's Word is no longer sufficient.

Satan used discontentment on Adam and Eve and remember this, they were living in Paradise, for goodness sake! When discontentment goes unchecked in our lives it will work like leaven does in bread, slowly breaking down our belief systems, allowing doubt to creep in and make the promises of God regarding our future seem insufficient. Then, we begin to rely on other means to secure our future. This seems to occur often in what our society calls a "mid-life crisis" and those, my friend, can be found in both men and women! When we fall into the temptation of discontentment, it always involves our integrity being compromised, and will easily leave our legacy tarnished.

OUR REMEDY FOR DISCONTENTMENT

I have some good news! We do have a remedy for discontentment, a way to gain victory at this Spiritual Front. It is found in Hebrews 12:1-2 (NLT):

> *"Therefore, since we are surrounded by such a huge crowd of witnesses to the life of faith, let us strip off every weight that slows us down, especially the sin that so easily trips us up. And let us run with endurance the*

race God has set before us. We do this by keeping our eyes on Jesus, the champion who initiates and perfects our faith. Because of the joy awaiting him, he endured the cross, disregarding its shame. Now he is seated in the place of honor beside God's throne."

We must stay focused on Him. Paul writes about his focus point in Philippians 3:14:

"I press toward the mark for the prize of the high calling of God in Christ Jesus."

Are you struggling to stay focused on Him? Start hanging around with focused people, get with good company, and loiter with some "FAT" people—you know, those who are **F**aithful, **A**vailable and **T**eachable to God! Paul shares with his "son in the gospel", Timothy, a key statement that effectively summarizes all that I've just written:

"But godliness with contentment is great gain."
1 Timothy 6:6

Godliness simply means we live our lives by walking in the Spirit, bearing much fruit. Faithfulness is being content to do what you are doing for God right now, and for the rest of your life, as you patiently wait for your next assignment. God is patient—He is not in a hurry. Unfaithfulness is one of the reasons why the promises of God are not being manifested in the lives of many believers. Yet faithfulness is the key to having the "finishing anointing". Anyone can have the *starting* anointing. Not everyone has the *finishing* anointing. The Apostle Paul did, as we read in 2 Timothy 4:7:

"I have fought a good fight, I have finished my course, I have kept the faith."

A FRESH ANOINTING IS A FINISHING ANOINTING

Keep your anointing fresh by having what I call "moments with Christ" throughout your day. Maintain a fresh, personal Word life and a fresh, personal prayer life and you will enjoy a fresh anointing.

I am fully persuaded that the older a believer grows in Christ, the more their anointing should increase, not decrease. If you do not believe this of yourself then you are leaking at this very moment! This is what we need to do every day of our lives:

"Draw nigh to God, and he will draw nigh to you…"
James 4:8a

It is a spiritual law that will never change for His children: Draw near, come close to Him and He promises that He will come close to you. What a God!

FOR PERSONAL REFLECTION OR DISCUSSION

- What assassin, or assassins, do you have to arrest in order to walk in victory?
- What are some of the rewards you've received in your life for walking in faithfulness?
- Have you been faithful to your friends?
- Do you surround yourself with faithful friends?
- Can you name people in your life who have set a standard for faithfulness?

DECLARATION

From this day forward, I have decided to walk in the faithfulness of Jesus Christ. It is my heart-filled desire to do so!

LET'S PRAY

Jesus, I know that You are aware of my lack of character in the arena of faithfulness. I know also that there is no condemnation to those who are in Christ Jesus, so thank You for not condemning me, but for encouraging me to move past my failures. I ask You for the spiritual strength to help me walk consistently. I do not want to be a broken tooth or a foot out of joint but, Lord, I want You, my spouse, my family, my boss and my pastor to have confidence in me. If You are for me then who can be against me? Thank You, Lord, for empowering me with Your faithfulness!
In Jesus' name, Amen.

CHAPTER TEN

MEEKNESS: GOD'S ANTIDOTE FOR PRIDE

WHEN SPEAKING about the fruit of the Spirit of meekness, we can never associate meekness with weakness. Moses was meek and we know what God accomplished in his life!

The fruit of the Spirit of meekness is the spiritual element we need to accomplish our assignment and arrive to our destiny. When infused with His character and the gifts that He has given us, nothing can or will stop us.

There is a thin line between pride and confidence. I like to call it "God-fidence"—yep, I really said it! I overheard someone once say, "I'm a humble person." What would be your first thought if you heard someone say that? I took a quick survey of about twenty people and they came to conclusion that it is a prideful statement. I thought that was interesting, but have you read this before?

> *"Now the man Moses was very meek (humble), above all the men which were upon the face of the earth."*
> **Numbers 12:3 (clarification mine)**

If you are familiar with the Old Testament writings you will know that it was Moses himself who wrote this. He alone did not write it. He actually penned it under the anointing of the Holy Spirit.

Most Christian Bible scholars are in agreement that the following Scriptures are referring to the rise and fall of our adversary Lucifer so I am sharing this only as a point of reference, not to glorify him in any way. However, I do believe that while knowing your enemy may be helpful, knowing God is *much more* important. Speaking prophetically of Lucifer, the Lord spoke this through Ezekiel:

> *"Son of man, take up a lamentation upon the king of Tyre, and say unto him, Thus saith the Lord God; Thou*

sealest up the sum, full of wisdom, and perfect in beauty. Thou hast been in Eden the garden of God; every precious stone was thy covering, the sardius, topaz, and the diamond, the beryl, the onyx, and the jasper, the sapphire, the emerald, and the carbuncle, and gold: the workmanship of thy tabrets and of thy pipes was prepared in thee in the day that thou wast created. Thou art the anointed cherub that covereth; and I have set thee so: thou wast upon the holy mountain of God; thou hast walked up and down in the midst of the stones of fire. Thou wast perfect in thy ways from the day that thou wast created, till iniquity was found in thee."
Ezekiel 28:12-15

As we just read, our enemy was once an angel made of precious stones and even tablets, tambourines and drums. Some scholars believe Lucifer was a literal, musical being because he was the covering cherub and the chief musician in heaven. This was until iniquity was found in him. What did he do? What was the iniquity? Well, let's read Isaiah 14:12-14:

"How art thou fallen from heaven, O Lucifer, son of the morning! How art thou cut down to the ground, which didst weaken the nations! For thou hast said in thine heart: I will ascend into heaven, I will exalt my throne above the stars of God: I will sit also upon the mount of the congregation, in the sides of the north: I will ascend above the heights of the clouds; I will be like the most High."

The five statements in the passage above are referred to as the five "I Wills" of Satan:

- I will ascend into heaven;

- I will exalt myself;

- I will sit upon the throne;

- I will ascend above;

- I will be like the Most High.

With these statements we can sum up the character of Satan in one word: *pride.* Pride is a powerful tool that stirs up the flesh of man more than any another. Mankind was first infected with the serpent's venom in the Garden of Eden when Adam and Eve wanted to have more in life than the paradise in which they lived. Because Jesus walked in humility and lived out the will of the Father, we are more than conquerors. That includes overcoming our pride.

I am not saying that you should tell everyone you meet that you are a humble person, but when you're walking in His anointing you can say things and write things that others cannot. I would, however, agree that it is always better for someone else to say that you are humble, or you might go through life saying, "I must be important cause I'm always thinking about myself."

In the book of Romans Paul gives us instruction concerning our own elevation of self:

"For I say, through the grace given unto me, to every man

*that is among you, not to think of himself more highly
than he ought to think; but to think soberly, according
as God hath dealt to every man the measure of faith."*
Romans 12:3

Paul is saying that we need to stop getting drunk on
ourselves! Humility occurs when we conform to the Word
of God. As Romans says:

*"And be not conformed to this world: but be ye
transformed by the renewing of your mind..."*
Romans 12:2a

Why? Because God is building something in you! Do
you want what *you* are building or do you want what God
wants to build in you?

*"For we are laborers together with God: ye are God's
husbandry, ye are God's building."*
1 Corinthians 3:9

When new houses are built the electricians put in new
wiring, and when it is installed the current should flow
throughout the whole house. Unfortunately, through
negligence or from having amateurs install your wiring,
sometimes things can become messy and wires can get
crossed, causing a short circuit. Electricians are
professionals—this is why you should have the wiring
checked before buying an older house. The same is

true in our walk with God. We need to have our wiring checked to be sure that our spiritual wires have not crossed over and short-circuited us into operating under the works of the flesh.

Developing the fruit of the Spirit is like the "wiring" of the Spirit. Believers should have a desire to develop His character in their lives. We do this when we purpose in our heart to yield to the Master Electrician. When a circuit does break, we just go back to the circuit box (the Bible), flick that switch (study it) and make the necessary adjustments in our lives to get the current of God's character flowing again. We must prepare by purposing in our hearts to yield to His character. Let's take a peek into the life of Daniel:

> *"But Daniel purposed in his heart that he would not defile himself with the portion of the king's meat, nor with the wine which he drank: therefore he requested of the prince of the eunuchs that he might not defile himself."*
> **Daniel 1:8**

Daniel was doing much more than a diet—it was about maintaining his godly character. Daniel and his friends had purposed in their hearts that they would not conform to the spirit of the heathen world into which they had been taken captive.

To my mind, to "purpose in your heart", like Daniel, is "to set or aim for an intentional goal for yourself". We must have absolutes in this chaotic world or we will end up like those lost in chaos and not walking in His character. A meek/humble person is someone who sees themselves soberly, as God sees them. To walk in pride is to promote or exalt ourselves at the expense of others.

After reading this hopefully you can see the main reason why God is so against pride, for Jesus could never gain something at the expense of others. Wouldn't that be sad, to intentionally exalt yourself at the expense of others? But it happens all the time, in the world and, sadly, in the church as well. Let's look at these three passages:

"Pride leads to disgrace, but with humility comes wisdom."
Proverbs 11:2 (NLT)

"Only by pride cometh contention..."
Proverbs 13:10a

Pride and arrogance will short circuit the anointing in your life.

"Pride goeth before destruction, and an haughty spirit before a fall."
Proverbs 16:18

Pride will always be evident in someone's life before their life comes crashing down.

THE STORY OF THE TWO DUCKS AND THE FROG

The story is told of two ducks and a frog who lived happily together in a farm pond. The best of friends they were. The three would amuse themselves and play together in their waterhole. When the hot, summer days came, however, the pond began to dry up, and soon it was evident they would have to move. This was no problem for the ducks who could easily fly to another pond. But the frog was stuck. So, it was decided that they would put a stick in the bill of each duck so the frog could hang onto it with his mouth as they flew to another pond. The plan worked well, so well, in fact, that as they were flying along a farmer looked up in admiration and mused, "Well, isn't that a clever idea! I wonder who thought of it?"

"I did", said the frog, and that was the end of the prideful frog. [50]

Did you know that God is training the meek to take over the earth? The Psalmist wrote:

"But the meek shall inherit the earth; and shall delight themselves in the abundance of peace."
Psalm 37:11

The world elevates the Brave Hearts, but our King

---

[50]   I found this story at https://bible.org/illustration/two-ducks-and-frog

elevates the *Humble* Hearts. The humble will inherit the earth because we yielded to meekness and learned to live from a position of humility. When we operate at the Spiritual Front of meekness, we yield to humility and touch heaven in order to change earth. When we learn humility, we learn the way of the Lord. Humility will open heaven, will open opportunities and open doors and will open your eyes to the things of God.

Listen, it doesn't matter what people think, it's what God thinks that matters! The sooner you become a God Pleaser and reject being a Man Pleaser the better off you, and everyone around you, will be.

Here are two quotes that I once heard to help you understand pride versus humility:

- Meekness or humility is dependence on GOD;

- Pride is dependence on SELF.

Why did God empower us with His meekness? God gave us meekness/humility as an antidote for our pride. Pride is the complete opposite of Jesus. We fight pride at the Spiritual Front of meekness. Pride is what Satan is all about. The pride of Satan was the venom that the serpent in the Garden injected when he bit mankind through Adam's disobedience. God will always resist a person who approaches Him in and with pride. He will, however, allow a meek and humble person to come into His presence. Peter sums it up this way:

"Likewise, ye younger, submit yourselves unto the elder. Yea, all of you be subject one to another, and be clothed with humility: for God resisteth the proud, and giveth grace to the humble."
1 Peter 5:5

Now here is the remedy:

"Humble yourselves therefore under the mighty hand of God (the authority of His Word and those in your life), that he may exalt you in due time: Casting all your care upon him; for he careth for you. Be sober, be vigilant; because your adversary the devil, as a roaring lion, walketh about, seeking whom he may devour: Whom resist stedfast in the faith, knowing that the same afflictions are accomplished in your brethren that are in the world."
1 Peter 5:6-9

A prideful person will promote "self" or their selfishness. A meek and humble person will seek to serve others. Prideful people have to prove themselves to others and you will notice they seem to try to top everyone's story. A meek and humble person waits patiently and quietly for God to vindicate them.

In closing, I would like to share a thought about two men in the Bible who held the same position. One was prideful and the other was meek and humble. The two men were King Saul and King David. They both have been noted for something they were seeking for:

- King Saul was known for seeking out donkeys and witches;
- King David was known as a man who sought God's heart.

The bigger question is: What will you be known for seeking?

FOR PERSONAL REFLECTION OR DISCUSSION

- Would you consider yourself a meek and humble person?
- Would your friends or spouse agree with you on your answer?
- Have you sensed pride rise up in your life recently?
- Did you catch it in time or did it take over a situation?
- Can you share an example in the Bible when Jesus showed meekness and humility?
- What made-up word did the author use to describe the thin line between pride and confidence? G_____!

DECLARATION

I declare, in the name of Jesus, that I will humble myself to You, Lord, today and to everyone I meet, but especially with my family.

LET'S PRAY

Father God, thank You so much for caring for me. Because of You I have an overcoming life being born again. I have access to Your meek and humble spirit with which You empowered me. When my flesh begins to rise up, I ask You to remind me of what You placed in me. Help me, Lord, to keep pride in check. Allow me to yield to meekness and humility even when I do not want to. Father, in Jesus' name, help me live a life of obedience, not because I have to but because I want to please You. Amen.

CHAPTER ELEVEN

GOVERNING YOUR UNDISCIPLINED SPIRIT

"This I say then, Walk in the Spirit, and ye shall not fulfil the lust of the flesh."

The Scripture above was written by Paul, in Galatians 5:16. I really like saying, "Walking in the Spirit"—it sounds so good to me when I hear myself saying these words. Because you are reading this, I am confident that you have a great desire to learn how to fight at each Spiritual Front and walk in the Spirit too. After seeing many Christian friends and ministers of the Gospel who have shipwrecked their lives by walking in the flesh, I know that I do not want that in my life, do you? It's because of this we can all sense that there is a great need for believers to learn how to walk in the Spirit.

Temperance, also known as self-control, is last on the list of the fruits of the Spirit (but by no means the least!) so allow me to pose these questions to you: Is it temperance that keeps us from getting too loose or lethargic in our walk with God? Is it what keeps us balanced in and unbalanced world? Is temperance, or self-control, something like when a person flexes their muscles? The dictionary says that *flex* means, "to move or tense by contraction."[51] It is a form of isometrics to help build muscle. My conclusion is that self-control will help keep us balanced and walking the disciplined line, and not get sloppy and inconsistent in our walk with God.

The word *temperance* means "self-control"[52], or another way one could say it would be "to control self." The root of *temperance* means "to soften or make mild so as to control."[53] A great example of this would be if someone slaps you in your emotional face and you refrain from

---

51 https://www.merriam-webster.com/dictionary/flex

52 https://www.dictionary.com/browse/temperance

53 https://www.merriam-webster.com/dictionary/temperance

retaliating—you've had your 'inner you' softened so that you can control your emotions and reactions more easily and carefully

Always keep in mind that we are free to choose any lifestyle we wish, but there are rewards or consequences for our choices. I will explain that further at the end of this chapter. I would like to remind you that we are talking about tempering our undisciplined spirit. Unfortunately, many Christians have no control over their spirit, soul, or body, and it can become confusing to people, both saved and unsaved.

If we are not walking in the Spirit, we are operating in the works of the flesh. This could be the reason why many of us have not felt the presence of God in our personal lives like we once did. The remedy would be that we must stop grieving His Spirit; we must repent and begin entertaining His presence once again.

My definition for a spiritual person is simply this: Someone who is governed by the Holy Spirit. The dictionary describes the word *govern* as "to control or be influenced by, to govern oneself, to conduct oneself, especially with regard to controlling one's emotions."[54]

That's a mouthful, isn't it? As believers we should be well aware that God doesn't control anyone, and He absolutely has no desire to do so. His true desire is that we learn to govern ourselves in this life. We do that by yielding to the authority and power of His word,

---

54 https://www.dictionary.com/browse/govern

bringing forth the fruit He has ordained for us to bear.

Please note that when someone has been truly born again, and has dedicated their life to God, these things should be evident in their life:

- There should be a noticeable change in the person through true repentance, and a change in attitude;
- There should be true transformation and change in their behavior;
- They will have a hunger for God;
- They will have a hunger for the holiness of God;
- They will possess a hatred for sin;
- They will love people.

If there is no change in the life of someone who says they have been born again, it can be confusing to others and to themselves. Even sinners know how Christians should live, because I tell you, as soon as you say or do something wrong they'll quickly say, "Hey, I thought you were a Christian!"

A born-again person must be able to govern his or her life from the inside out. Before someone can have victory in their public life they must learn to govern their private life. The key to the power of a changed life lies within the regenerated (born-again) human spirit. When the Holy Spirit comes into our hearts, at the time of our conversion to Christ, He changes our dead, sinful, undisciplined spirit and makes it alive to the things of

God. Can somebody say, "Thank God I'm saved!"? Again, I would like to share this ever-important spiritual truth of the new birth with you. When you are saved God doesn't empower your old character, but rather He empowers you with *His* character. Your old character is dead and the best thing you can do is to reckon yourself dead and crucified to the world, and the world to you, as it says in Romans 6:11 and Galatians 6:14. You may have to declare those verses out loud every day, until faith comes.

I am so thankful that I had the revelation years ago that Christianity is not about a bunch of rules and regulations, but rather that it is about empowerment. That means our God empowers the human spirit to enable us to live and reign with Him in our lifetime and beyond. *Empowerment* means "to give power or authority to."[55] God has empowered us to overcome sin and shame and produce the character of His Son, Jesus.

As I said earlier in this book, when you are tested or tempted you will always be tempted and tested in one of the nine fruits of the Spirit. That is why I call them the nine Spiritual Fronts of the Spirit. 1 Corinthians 10:13 teaches us that:

> *"There hath no temptation taken you but such as is common to man: but God is faithful, who will not suffer you to be tempted above that ye are able; but will*

---

55 https://www.dictionary.com/browse/empowerment

with the temptation also make a way to escape, that ye may be able to bear it."

Did you know God has put a treasure in us?

"But we have this treasure in earthen vessels, that the excellency of the power may be of God, and not of us."
2 Corinthians 4:7

What's interesting is that the Greek word for *treasure* is *thēsaurós*[56], which is where we get the English word *thesaurus*. A thesaurus is a book loaded with synonyms that provide a deeper look into other definitions of one word. So the treasure that God put in us, deep within our heart/spirit, is made manifest to us as we go deeper in Him and that will 1) supply all we need and 2) define who we really are. This is all made possible by who we are joined together with. Paul wrote:

"But the person who is joined to the Lord is one spirit with him."
1 Corinthians 6:17 (NLT)

This joint union is the greatest union in the universe—the fusion of our spirit with His Holy Spirit. There is no other fusion available or more powerful to be found. If you will learn to yield to the Holy Spirit then the

---

56 https://www.dictionary.com/browse/thesaurus

anointing on your life will remain fresh. Of course, reading and studying the Word helps, and praying is also a great discipline, but if you do not yield to His Spirit and produce His character through obedience, you and I will be missing the mark. We must not just be hearers of the Word, but doers of the Word, and bearing the fruit of change is being a doer.

I just mentioned the anointing and character so let's look into a story concerning a very interesting person, who by the way is my favorite apostle, the Apostle Paul. To me, Paul is another example of a changed life. His transformation was so powerful and so sincere that the anointing on him was unlike anything we have seen in our present time. In Paul's day, people were coming back from the dead and folks with sicknesses and diseases were being healed. Some folks were even healed by cloths that he prayed over! This happened while he himself suffered beyond what any other human, besides Jesus Himself, had to bear for the sake of the gospel.

His anointing put the "shock and awe" in the hearts of people. Here, in Acts 24:25 we read that when:

"And as he reasoned of righteousness, temperance, and judgment to come, Felix trembled, and answered, Go thy way for this time; when I have a convenient season, I will call for thee."

I love reading this! The Spirit of God flows through

Paul and the anointing causes conviction of sin on Felix. The way I think of it, Felix began to feel like a blind cat in a room filled with rocking chairs! The Bible says he trembled, which means he was in fear and alarmed in his heart. Oh, that precious anointing!

Here is a little recap from a previous chapter, "The Main Ingredient". The Word was written in divine order for a reason, it was not written in random thoughts. It was line upon line, precept upon precept. I believe the fruit of the Spirit was also written in divine order. Love was listed first because it was the main ingredient, or the most important virtue according to 1 Corinthians 13:13. If you are determined to walk in love the rest of the fruit can follow through with the lesser amount of resistance. As you know, it is His love not our love.

Take a look at the illustration of the human being in three parts.

When the Lord Jesus reigns as Lord in your spirit (heart), your spirit (heart) has the ability to tell your soul (mind) what to think, and then your soul (mind) tells your body what to do, so it is like this:

- Jesus is Lord of your spirit;

- Spirit controls your mind;

- Mind controls your body.

This second illustration breaks it down more, but keep in mind that the soul is made up of your mind, intellect, emotions and will:

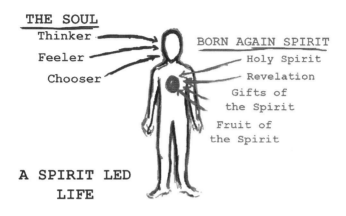

The soul is the Thinker (mind), the Feeler (emotion) and the Chooser (will). The spirit-ruled person (born again and governed by spirit) has the Holy Spirit living and governing within and this is where you receive revelation by the Spirit because this is where God speaks to you.

One of my favorite Scriptures on hearing the voice of God is found in Proverbs 20:27:

"The spirit of man is the candle of the LORD, searching all the inward parts of the belly."

Walking in the Spirit is a spirit-governed life. It's not a perfect life, but rather it is a life striving for perfection (maturity). God has given us the ability to stay in control of our lives as 2 Timothy 1:7 (NLT) says:

"For God has not given us a spirit of fear and timidity, but of power, love, and self-discipline."

Now, according to this next Scripture, we will see that temperance or self-control is one of the ingredients which, when added into our lives, will help us to never fall or fail. As Peter says:

"Grace and peace be multiplied unto you through the knowledge of God, and of Jesus our Lord, According as his divine power hath given unto us all things that pertain unto life and godliness, through the knowledge of him that hath called us to glory and virtue: Whereby are given unto us exceeding great and precious promises: that by these ye might be partakers of the divine nature, having escaped the corruption that is in the world through lust. And beside this, giving all diligence, add to your faith virtue; and to virtue knowledge; And to knowledge temperance; and to temperance patience; and to patience godliness; And to godliness brotherly kindness; and to brotherly kindness charity. For if these things be in you, and abound, they make you that ye shall neither be barren nor unfruitful in the knowledge of our Lord Jesus Christ. But he that lacketh these things is blind, and cannot see afar off, and hath forgotten that he was purged from his old sins. Wherefore the rather, brethren, give diligence to make your calling and election sure: for if ye do these things, ye shall never fall."
2 Peter 1:2-10

That doesn't mean you will not sin or miss God at times, but I feel that it is similar to what was said about Abraham, that he, "staggered not at the promise of God through unbelief; but was strong in faith." (Romans 4:20) We, like Abraham, cannot separate ourselves from the promises that God has given us—even when we fail.

As ministers of the gospel (and I am referring to every minister of reconciliation, which includes everyone who is born again) we have to make sure that we live a self-controlled, disciplined life. Paul is an example as he writes in 1 Corinthians 9:27 (AMPC):

> *"But [like a boxer] I buffet my body [handle it roughly, discipline it by hardships] and subdue it, for fear that after proclaiming to others the Gospel and things pertaining to it, I myself should become unfit [not stand the test, be unapproved and rejected as a counterfeit."*

Wow, that is good! Paul's brother in Christ, Peter, also thought the same when he said it in 1 Peter 1:13a (NLT):

> *"So prepare your minds for action and exercise self-control…"*

Paul told the Corinthians:

> *"And I, brethren, could not speak unto you as unto spiritual, but as unto carnal, even as unto babes in*

*Christ. I have fed you with milk, and not with meat:
for hitherto ye were not able to bear it, neither yet now
are ye able. For ye are yet carnal: for whereas there is
among you envying, and strife, and divisions, are ye not
carnal, and walk as men?"*
1 Corinthians 3:1-3

You know, living a Christian life is simply impossible—without the Holy Spirit, that is! Please keep this in mind that Jesus would never command us to do something that He wouldn't help us with. One thing I do know is that it will be worth it and it is good to know that God is a rewarder in this life and beyond.

FOR PERSONAL REFLECTION OR DISCUSSION

- What in the world have you been doing?
- Have you changed since the day you received Christ, and how?
- What would your friends and family say about your character if asked?
- Would you be convicted in a court of law for being a Christian?
- Are you ready to meet Jesus?
- Why or why not?

DECLARATION

From this day forward, I have decided to make a

decision to change in the following areas of my character:

_____

_____

_____

_____

_____

_____

_____

_____

_____

LET'S PRAY

Father, I am so thankful to You for sending Jesus to die on the cross for my sins. Thank You so much for saving me and for all that You have done in my life. Now, Lord, I ask You with a sincere heart to allow Your Holy Spirit to work on the areas that I have written down. I know that the character that I need is in me—it's Your character that You have empowered me with. Lord, from this day forward I will, by the grace of God, yield to what You have put in me when temptation, tests and trials come my way. In Your righteous name, Jesus, I pray. Amen, and amen.

CHAPTER TWELVE

SO ARE YOU ACTING HUMAN AGAIN?

A LLOW ME to give a solid. By that I mean some solid advice that can last a lifetime—something that you can hang on to when your world seems to be falling about, something you can always depend on in times of trouble: Change is inevitable. Yet even if people change, countries change, philosophies change but God never changes. He even says so Himself:

"I am the LORD, I change not…"
Malachi 3:6a

The writer of Hebrews elaborates in Hebrews 13:8-9a (NIV):

"Jesus Christ is the same yesterday and today and forever. Do not be carried away by all kinds of strange teachings…"

God doesn't change and neither does His Word. If you haven't taken the time to stop and read the cultural landscape or mindset of our society I would advise you to do so—you will notice that this world's philosophy is changing, very quickly.

Proof in point, I overheard this statement recently, by someone who said, "Truth is determined these days when the majority of society believe something to be true." That, my friend, is quite unsettling and chilling—especially to us, the Body of Christ, who have been called, sanctified and ordained to go and bear much fruit and be that shining light to the world and the salt of the earth with His truth.

The moral compass of this world is changing as fast as the wild spinning compass of the fictional character Capt. Jack Sparrow, in the Disney film series *Pirates of the Caribbean.* His crazy compass was always changing, spinning around as the desires of his heart flipped from one thing to another, and never giving any clear direction. And you know what? Captain Jack still put great faith in it, just like many people today put their trust in godless people. These people, with a fluctuating moral compass like Captain Jack's, are leading the way for moral change in the seven "Pillars of Society" in which we and our children live. And now, if that isn't sad enough, modern society is screaming at the Church and demanding that we conform to this world's philosophy and version of truth. But God's Word instructs us:

> *"And be not conformed to this world: but be ye transformed by the renewing of your mind, that ye may prove what is that good, and acceptable, and perfect, will of God."*
> **Romans 12:2**

MERE HUMANS?

Do you really want "mere humans" to dictate the direction of your moral compass? I know that may sound condescending and disempowering but allow me to explain the term "mere humans".

"Well, I'm only human after all." You may have heard yourself or others make a similar statement like that before. This is said usually after someone has made a mistake or repeatedly made the same mistake. It would be an accurate response if we were trying to learn to do a backflip or play an musical instrument, or learning to play the game of golf.

What I am referring to is when we, born-again believers,

behave immorally and hurt the people we love through living a lie and with constantly bad behavior—and we just shrug our shoulders and say, "Well, I'm only human after all, you know, so don't judge me." It may be understandable if we were talking about someone who didn't know God, but we are God's children. Saying, "I'm only human, you know" may make you feel good but it is counterproductive to your walk with God—and it would not hold up in court. I'm not talking about the court downtown, I'm talking about His Supreme Court—the court of the Judgment Seat of Christ for those of us who are saved.

This is where our lives flash before us as we give an account of the moments, days or even years that we have lived and operated as "mere humans" as well as the times we lived in the full potential of what God put in us.

HEAVENLY REWARDS

Here on earth we may receive awards for our accomplishments but God promises us heavenly rewards. He is a rewarded not a withholder, as some have come to believe.

Let me ask you this question: How important do you think godly character is to God? Be assured that when you die and go to heaven you are not taking your fancy clothes, your high fashion purses or your fancy car. I'm going to keep going: neither are you taking your bank account, your degrees, your career, your top sales reward and definitely not your smart phone or your smart watch, or even your so-called ministry!

Listen, my friend, the only thing you will bring to heaven is your character and how you treated people. The Apostle Paul looked into the future for us and warns us of the Judgment Seat of Christ in 2 Corinthians 5:10b:

> *"…That every one may receive the things done in his body, according to that he hath done, whether it be good or bad."*

He also wrote:

> *"…For we shall all stand before the judgment seat of Christ."*
> **Romans 14:10b**

Paul is writing to the church in Corinth that was birthed toward the end of his second missionary journey. He, being the spiritual father of the ministry, had a voice into their hearts and strongly exhorts them to keep their eyes opened to gospel truth.

> *"You are still worldly. For since there is jealousy and quarreling among you, are you not worldly? Are you not acting like mere humans?"*
> **1 Corinthians 3: 3 (NIV)**

*"For you are still controlled by your sinful nature. You
are jealous of one another and quarrel with each other.
Doesn't that prove you are controlled by your sinful
nature? Aren't you living like people of the world?"*
1 Corinthians 3: 3 (NLT)

*"For you are still carnal. For where there are envy,
strife, and divisions among you, are you not carnal and
behaving like mere men?"*
1 Corinthians 3: 3 (NKJV)

So, Mr. and Mrs. Saint, have you been "acting as a
mere human" again? Have you slipped back into old
fleshly, carnal habits? Seriously, aren't you tired of
making up excuses for your actions? Now you're born
again you should no longer consider yourself a "mere
human being"—rather you have become a powerful
spiritual being, a new creation, someone who has never
existed before except in the mind of God. 2 Corinthians
5:16-17 (NLT) says you are:

*"So we have stopped evaluating others from a human point
of view. At one time we thought of Christ merely from a
human point of view. How differently we know him now!
This means that anyone who belongs to Christ has become
a new person. The old life is gone; a new life has begun!"*

So stop saying, "I'm just a janitor", "I'm just a stay-
at-home Mom", "I am just human". Listen, you are an

on-fire, born-again, Holy Ghost-filled, devil-crushing janitor/stay-at-home Mom/Human. Stop making excuses—it is stunting your growth!

For us to grow up spiritually we need to stop making excuses about our lack of godly character and moral deficiency—especially because God has empowered you with His character, the fruit of the Spirit. Excuses are malignant to your spiritual development. They will weaken your Spiritual Fronts and will hinder you on your journey of becoming an overcoming Christian. You have to pause and ask yourself, "Isn't time that I grew up spiritually?"

"When I was a child, I spoke and thought and reasoned as a child. But when I grew up, I put away childish things."
1 Corinthians 13:11 (NLT)

In my weak moments I remind myself that God did not empower my character but rather He empowered me with His character. I remind myself to yield to what He put in me. Hopefully you can see now that you really have no excuse when you have God on the inside of you!

Imagine a PostIt note on your forehead that says, "I've got God on the inside." Whenever you look in a mirror you see it, and it should stir up your memory of Who is inside of you. "Danny, do you *really* mean that God is on the inside of me?" Yep, that's right—God is on the inside of you because that's what happens when you believe that Jesus is the Son of God. Now don't just set there staring in wonder about it—live it out. Even Jesus said it:

> *"Marvel not that I said unto thee, Ye must be born again."*
> *John 3:7*

Allow me to explain how God got inside of you. Let's zoom in on a conversation between Jesus and a very religious man named Nicodemus:

> *"There was a man of the Pharisees, named Nicodemus, a ruler of the Jews: The same came to Jesus by night, and said unto him, Rabbi, we know that thou art a teacher come from God: for no man can do these miracles that thou doest, except God be with him."*
> *John 3:1-2*

I'd like to make a side observation here. I have heard some people say that Jesus didn't answer Nicodemus's question. Well, because Nicodemus was talking about "coming from God", I believe Jesus does answer him by explaining how someone could "come from God". Let's continue:

> *"Jesus answered and said unto him, Verily, verily, I say unto thee, Except a man be born again, he cannot see the kingdom of God."*
> *John 3:3*

So Jesus is saying that for someone to see or experience the kingdom of God they must be born again. Let's do a quick word study here. The word *born* is the Greek word *gennaō*[57], derived from the word *genos*[58], from which we get our English word *gene*. In case you didn't know, our genes are what biologically make us "us" and are passed on to us from our earthly parents. The word *again* in the Greek means "from above or anew."[59]

> *"Nicodemus saith unto him, How can a man be born when he is old? can he enter the second time into his mother's womb, and be born?"*
> **John 3:4**

One Sunday we had an older doctor attending our church and I paused from preaching on this passage and got his medical opinion. He confirmed that it would be impossible for me, or anyone for that matter, to go back into their mother's womb again and be born again. Of course, I did it for humor's sake, but it is true. Let's read Jesus response to Nicodemus:

> *"Jesus answered, Verily, verily, I say unto thee, Except a man be born of water and of the Spirit, he cannot enter into the kingdom of God. That which is born of the*

---

57 Strong's reference: 1080, *gennaó*

58 Strong's reference: 1085, *geno*

59 Strong's reference: 509, *anóthen*

flesh is flesh; and that which is born of the Spirit is spirit."
John 3:5-6

Here Jesus explains the difference between the two births. "What is flesh is flesh" is referring to our *natural* birth and "That which is born of the Spirit is spirit" refers to our *spiritual* birth—the New Birth. The natural will never be supernatural, and the supernatural will never be natural. This is vital for us to remember: at our conversion God did not empower us with weakness— natural flesh—but rather He empowered us with Himself and with His strength.

"For God has not given us a spirit of fear and timidity, but of power, love, and self-discipline."
2 Timothy 1:7 (NLT)

I honestly believe that the new birth has been underrated, mostly because it has been misunderstood, maybe even overlooked, among Christians. With that in mind let's have some fun and raise the bar to challenge ourselves.

Let's imagine for a moment that you have decided to live a "no excuse" life. Wow, that would affect *every single* area of your life, wouldn't it? Your spirit, soul and body; from your heart to your education; from where you are now to financial security; from feeling lonely and useless to living a fulfilled life. When you choose to live a "no excuse" life you stir up God in you.

The word *excuse*, when used as a verb, means "your attempt to lessen the blame or to defend or justify an action you took." When you use the word *excuse* as a noun you are using it as "a reason or explanation to defend or justify a fault or offense."[60]

> *"An excuse is worse than a lie when you use it to hide from yourself; for an excuse is a lie guarded."*
> **Alexander Pope, 18th-century poet**

Imagine for a moment that you're living that "no excuse" life—how it would improve your life, your health and your walk with God? The omnipotent power of God is released from the inside of you into action. *Omni* means "all, the whole, of every kind, everything"[61] and *potent* means "powerful, mighty"[62], so you and I have all, complete—unlimited, even—power and influence in this world if we will "JUST DO IT!"

God is omnipotent and He is living on the inside of you. All we have to do is tap into it to find the will of God and take the steps of faith necessary, then He will release His power through us and guide us in every assignment of our lives.

> *"And Jesus looking upon them saith, With men it is*

---

60 https://www.dictionary.com/browse/excuse

61 http://www.latin-dictionary.net/search/latin/omni

62 https://www.dictionary.com/browse/potent

impossible, but not with God: for with God all things are possible."
Mark 10:27

Okay, I now dub you a "Person of Possibilities". What is even better is that God has called you His Son or Daughter, and nothing—absolutely nothing—shall be impossible for you in all that He has called you to do.

As I close, I would like to share with you some things that will cause you to think or examine yourself in the faith. It has to do with rewards, here on earth, and after our "earthly visit".

In John 15:16 Jesus says:

"Ye have not chosen Me, but I have chosen you, and ordained you, that ye should go and bring forth fruit, and that your fruit should remain: that whatsoever ye shall ask of the Father in my name, He may give it you."

Did you read that? We will receive *more* answered prayer!

Sinners who are lost will stand before the white throne judgment and be condemned to the second death in the Lake of Fire with Satan and the dragon. But saints (those who are saved) will stand before the Judgment Seat of Christ and be purified by a holy fire before they enter. Some will receive rewards and other will suffer losses but thank God they are saved!

> *"Now if any man build upon this foundation gold, silver, precious stones, wood, hay, stubble; Every man's work shall be made manifest: for the day shall declare it, because it shall be revealed by fire; and the fire shall try every man's work of what sort it is. If any man's work abide which he hath built thereupon, he shall receive a reward. If any man's work shall be burned, he shall suffer loss: but he himself shall be saved; yet so as by fire."*
> *1 Corinthians 3:12-15*

Lastly, Peter wanted us to remember something in the first chapter of his first epistle:

> *"And remember that the heavenly Father to whom you pray has no favorites. He will judge or reward you according to what you do. So you must live in reverent fear of him during your time here as 'temporary residents'."*
> *1 Peter 1:17 (NLT)*

FOR PERSONAL REFLECTION OR DISCUSSION

- What are some so-called truths you have made up?
- Do you understand the "mere humans" statement now? Explain.
- Have you thrown away Capt. Jack's moral compass yet?
- Does living a "no excuse" life excite you?

- Or have you decided to continue to make excuses the rest of your life?
- Are you ready for the Judgement Seat of Christ? If not, what changes do you plan on making to enrich your life?

DECLARATION

I declare today that I will begin to live a "no excuse" life.

LET'S PRAY

Father, I so love and appreciate what You have done for me. You have given Your only Son, Jesus, to die for me so I can live with You forever—not just in heaven but here on earth. I repent for living a careless life and not considering that my days here are short. I am so sorry for not loving and caring for people the way Jesus taught. I am sorry for not yielding to Your character that you have empowered me with. You have been so merciful to me. I choose not to conform to this world, but I will be transformed by the renewing of my mind. I have a desire to change and to live a life that will be rewarded at the Judgement Seat of Christ. Lord, please continue to remind me to not seek the approval of man but know that my reward will be giving glory always to you.
Amen

ABOUT THE AUTHOR

I N THE early 1980's Danny Thornton worked the streets of Syracuse as an Evangelist. It was the early days of his ministry as a street preacher, and outreach director, and he also had a radio outreach program, all while he faithfully served as an assistant to his pastor, James Farley of Calvary Church (now Family Worship Center) in Clay, NY, for eleven years. In June of 1990 Danny and his wife, Jean, were released to pioneer an inner-city church in the heart of Syracuse. Against all odds, River Church (aka Solid Rock) flourished and became one of the most respected ministries to serve the people of the Syracuse Metro area. During this time the church was credited by Syracuse Food Bank for having served up to one million meals in one year.

Danny, through his dynamic charisma, has invested his life in evangelizing a lost world for the gospel of Jesus Christ. He is a conference preacher, ministering across the USA, from New York to California, and internationally. He is a disciple-making pastor with a passion to reach the lost and hurting, and to teach and raise up leaders.

Danny married his high school sweetheart, Jean Marie, and they have been married for forty-six years (and counting!). But what they are most proud of, and thankful for, is their family of two lovely daughters, two fine son-in-laws, and six grandchildren who all have a relationship with God and are serving in their church. Danny and Jean have been the Lead Pastors of RIVER CHURCH now for twenty-eight years. Danny is also the Founder of GODSTRENGTH.COACH MINISTRIES, INC. which provides: ministry to men; evangelism training (street, lifestyle and power); one-on-one personal coaching, short- and long-term; marriage guidance; personal life change through pastoral care; discipleship training and tools, and how to use them; leadership training; and ministry/church consulting.

Consider inviting Danny for Sunday or weekday services or conferences: **info@godstrength.coach** or visit **http://godstrength.coach**.

PRAYER

WE HOPE you enjoyed this book and that it has been both a blessing and a challenge to your life and walk with God. Maybe you just got hold of it and are glancing through before starting. We made the decision as a publishing company right from the start never to take for granted that everyone has prayed a prayer to receive Jesus as their Lord, so we are including that as the finale to this book. If you have never asked Jesus into your life and would like to do that now, it's so easy. Just pray this simple prayer:

Dear Lord Jesus,
Thank You for dying on the cross for me. I believe
that You gave Your life so that I could have life.
When You died on the cross, You died as an
innocent man who had done nothing wrong. You

*were paying for my sins and the debt I could never
pay. I believe in You, Jesus, and receive the brand
new life and fresh start that the Bible promises that
I can have. Thank You for my sins forgiven, for the
righteousness that comes to me as a gift from You,
for hope and love beyond what I have known and
the assurance of eternal life that is now mine.
Amen.*

Good next moves are to get yourself a Bible that is
easy to understand and begin to read. Maybe start in
John so you can discover all about Jesus for yourself.
Start to pray—prayer is simply talking to God—and,
finally, find a church that's alive and get your life
planted in it. These simple ingredients will cause your
relationship with God to grow.

Why not email us and let us know if you did that so
we can rejoice with you?

The Great Big Life Publishing team
info@greatbiglifepublishing.com

FURTHER INFORMATION

FOR FURTHER information about the author of this book, or to order more copies, please contact:

Great Big Life Publishing
Empower Centre
83-87 Kingston Road
Portsmouth
Hampshire
PO2 7DX
United Kingdom
info@greatbiglifepublishing.com

Or visit our website: greatbiglifepublishing.com.

ARE YOU AN AUTHOR?

DO YOU have a word from God on your heart that you're looking to get published to a wider audience?

We're looking for manuscripts that identify with our own vision of bringing life-giving and relevant messages to Body of Christ. Send yours for review towards possible publication to:

Great Big Life Publishing
Empower Centre
83-87 Kingston Road
Portsmouth
Hampshire, PO2 7DX
United Kingdom
info@greatbiglifepublishing.com

Printed in Poland
by Amazon Fulfillment
Poland Sp. z o.o., Wrocław

36902649R00121